# THE 21st century MANAGER

# THE 21st century MANAGER

## future-focused skills
### for the next millennium

## DI KAMP

**KOGAN PAGE**

YOURS TO HAVE AND TO HOLD
BUT NOT TO COPY

First published 1999

Reprinted 1999

Kogan Page Limited
120 Pentonville Road
London
N1 9JN
UK

Kogan Page Limited
163 Central Avenue, Suite 4
Dover
NH 03820
USA

**British Library Cataloguing in Publication Data**

A CIP record for this book is available from the British Library.

ISBN 0 7494 2950 X

Typeset by JS Typesetting, Wellingborough, Northants
Printed and bound in Great Britain by Biddles Ltd, Guildford and King's Lynn

# contents

# acknowledgements

This book is based on work I have done with many managers over the years. I want to acknowledge their contributions, through their input and their questions.

I also want to recognize my teachers, who have inspired me and made me think deeply about this subject, through their seminars, books and tapes. Someone once said that there is no such thing as an original thought, and I know that I have absorbed many of the wise thoughts of others into my work over the years.

My thanks to John Hume who patiently transferred the script to computer and noticed where my writing didn't make sense.

And finally thanks to Terry Hodgetts, who read the script and commented most usefully, from a manager's perspective.

# introduction

I was prompted to write this book by the work I do training and facilitating the development of managers. It is based on what I hear managers say they need to help them make sense of the multitude of theories and 'new' ideas they are presented with. The process the book follows in its format is a proven one in live workshops, taking the manager through a carefully thought through process to become a 21st century manager.

This book has been written to deal with the 'how' of being a 21st century manager, rather than just the 'what'. It takes some of the themes that have been emphasized in other books and develops the methods that managers can use which will help them to move from their present position to one that is closer to the ideal.

I assume that most managers have accepted intellectually that there is a need for a change in style, but have not yet come to terms with how they put the changes into practice, when they are busy trying to make things work as they stand.

The book emphasizes the familiarity of the concepts, and gives simple activities to help managers to revise their way of thinking about their own development and to gently introduce new practice in their way of working.

There is also a reading list for those who want to know more about any particular aspect of management that is only covered briefly within the book.

There are numerous examples to illustrate the points made, and the book is designed to be readable and practical rather than adding to the existing theoretical works.

Please enjoy reading through this book. Use what seems useful to you, ignore what doesn't. You will recognize much of the material – it is only common good practice after all. I hope there are also pieces that will make you stop and think – none of us has reached the stage of having finished our development, if we truly want to be 21st century managers.

Di Kamp
6 Oaklands, Cradley, Malvern, Worcs. WR13 5LA, England, 1999
Tel: (44) 1886 880716     e-mail: di.kamp@virgin.net

# Part I

# The Overview

# the **context**

You don't need to be told again. You already know that changes in working practice for managers are inevitable. You have received this message from the management gurus – Tom Peters, Charles Handy, Peter Senge and others – for several years now. The likelihood is that your organization has changed or developed its mission statement and its organizational policy to reflect the required changes. And you have probably had to make some changes already, maybe adjusting to down-sizing, or having your role redefined.

However, knowing intellectually that change is inevitable is very different from embracing and actioning that change. Moving from knowing about to doing is much more difficult, especially when there doesn't seem to be a lot of evidence around you that radical change is *really* required. Most organizations I visit are struggling with how to make the changes really work, or have just paid lip service to changes and carried on as they always did. The history of working practice is very strong, and there is not enough evidence that change is really necessary. After all, we are used to 'fire-fighting', dealing with a crisis when it is upon us, rather than planning for a different future.

Change is something we tend not to plan for. We just deal with it when it becomes inevitable. Yet the changes that are already evident in working practice are major and need forethought. This is truly doing something different, and intellectual acceptance is not enough. We need to get hearts and souls involved.

## so what is really happening?

There are some changes in working practice which are already widespread. Most organizations have:

■ delayered, down-sized, or whatever they have called it. There are now fewer managers with more responsibility;
■ become more customer-focused. This will often be expressed in the company mission statement and by such things as customer surveys; customer focus teams have become more common;

- introduced more flexible working patterns for employees. This may mean multi-skilling the workforce, working in teams, flexible hours, or even working from home;
- looked at empowering the workforce. This proposes decisions are taken at the point of action, that everyone is accountable and responsible for their own work, and that employees are involved in the continuous improvement of the business.

*How has your organization changed over the last few years? Perhaps you have re-written your mission statement, or produced one, or reorganized your employees into teams. Identify the ways your organization has moved towards these ideas.*

However, when you look beyond the rhetoric at the everyday practice in organizations, at how people actually do their work, then the story is very different:

- Most people are stretched to their limit, working hard to try to fulfil their increased responsibilities.
- Few people feel really valued or empowered by their organization. More commonly they feel put upon and threatened. Where the idea of empowerment has been introduced, it is often with no preparation or training and no clear parameters.
- Customer focus is often given less priority than short-term cost object-ives in the organization, and pleasing the boss comes before pleasing the customer. Excuses are found for poor performance in customer surveys, or there are patchy improvements that don't take too much effort, such as customer guarantees with lots of provisos.
- Team-working translates into individuals put together in a group but still trying to prove their individual worth, in competition with the rest of their 'team', because the reward systems in the organization still reward individuals rather than team effort.
- Employees have responsibility but not authority. They still have to check decisions with line managers and let them have the final word, because they have discovered that empowerment means getting the blame when something doesn't work in the way that the manager expected it to.
- Few people suggest radical or innovative changes in working processes, in case they don't work. Anyway they notice that generally managers don't want them to suggest changes – they prefer to be in charge and seen as the expert themselves.
- Managers are still controlling and directing the workforce, because they haven't really learned how to do anything different and fear the

consequences of letting go of that control. As one manager said to me, 'It will lead to anarchy.'

- Individuals are blamed for mistakes and failures, so play safe as much as they can.
- Most people do not trust management or the organization to treat them fairly or well. They treat with cynicism such statements as 'People are our greatest asset', or core values that state that the organization values its people, because they still see managers having favourites, or dismissing their concerns.
- Most people feel insecure in their jobs. The constant restructuring of organizations has led to no one feeling that they are secure, so they keep their heads down, work hard, and hope that they will not be in the next batch of redundancies.

Does this sound depressingly familiar to you? Work has not been generally regarded as something to enjoy or be fulfilled by. It comes as no surprise to most people that the changes in working practice have not led to an enhanced sense of fulfilment or self-worth, often just the opposite.

*Does any of this apply to your organization? To what extent? Look again at this list and do an honest assessment of the present state of your organization.*

## why is this so?

There is a cultural history of work in industrial societies which most of us have absorbed. Our expectations are coloured by what we have been told about work, through books, through film, through all the media – and perhaps most importantly, through our parents and other relations.

The generalized picture given is that it is something you have to do to earn your living. You work hard, you try to avoid being too exploited by your bosses or getting into trouble, and you compensate for it in your leisure time. This may sound too harsh, yet it is the picture that many have of what work is like. And this is still perpetuated. Ask people if they enjoy their work, and the number who say they do is far outweighed by those who find it more frustrating or wearing than fulfilling.

## the theory behind the changes

When changes to working practice were first proposed by the business theorists, the intention was to produce a very different result.

I remember hearing inspired speeches describing how advances in technology would transform the workplace, taking away the drudgery of most jobs and enabling people to use their creativity at work. It was also clear to such theorists that people would need to work fewer hours and would have more time and energy to develop their talents in different directions. The implications of such visions, in terms of how people were educated, how people earned their living and how everyone was given a chance to share in the improved way of life were enormous.

It required a new definition of work, a radical shift in the type of education, and revolutionary changes in policies on tax, how wages are paid, etc. Without these other changes, the effect of technological change would be very different. If we didn't prepare people properly for the change of lifestyle and change of working practice, then we wouldn't be able to use the opportunity well. And if we didn't change the systems of reward and taxation, then we would not be reflecting the change in other areas.

From those original theories on the effect of technology, further theories on work practice were developed. They emphasized the importance of developing a way of distinguishing products and services through quality, and pointed out that it would no longer be possible to achieve that by developing something that no one else could do. Technology would mean that anything could be replicated by others very quickly and unique products would be a thing of the past. Consequently the difference would be in the level of customer service, the consistency of quality, and the efficiency of the processes used. All these are dependent on how people behave in their job. If they believe in what they are producing and are allowed to contribute fully, then that will result in the differentiating factors.

From this set of theories were adopted such strategies as Total Quality Management, Business Process Re-engineering, Customer Focus, Empowerment, Self-Managed Teams, and so on.

Again, though, there were parts of the theory that were largely ignored, such as the need to train people consistently and invest in their development, the need to change policies on reward and recognition, and the need to ensure genuine commitment from employees by encouraging their full involvement in decision-making.

## what has actually happened

We are living with the effects of a clash of paradigms. We have introduced some of the elements of the different working practice envisioned by the theorists while maintaining large chunks of the traditional view of work. This means that neither paradigm works properly.

Traditional working practice has gone. Technology has replaced the need for much traditional labour.

I remember 20 years ago visiting the Cadbury chocolate factory and being shown the two new machines they had installed. The guide announced proudly, 'These two machines have taken over the work of 40 people, and only require one person per shift to keep an eye on them. They also work 24 hours a day, seven days a week, 52 weeks a year, as opposed to the more limited hours we could expect from people.' My thought was, what happens to all the people who no longer have a job? Even if there were re-training to look after the machines, that still leaves 34 people without a job.

As well as the obvious changes that come with technological advances in machinery and equipment, there are the changes that result from adopting another part of the vision of a different working practice where people in work are empowered to make decisions and use their creativity. An element of this part of the vision was a reduced need for management control and an increase in the range of work people undertook. There tends to be less of a management hierarchy and there are more multi-functional teams fulfilling a variety of work objectives.

However, the investment in training people to work differently so that these new roles work well has often been minimal. Such a radical change requires a lot of support and reinforcement and in many companies such a long-term view was not taken. The old concept of 'profit now' has largely been maintained and the reduction in people employed has been seen as convenient cost cutting rather than requiring important long-term development for those remaining. So people have tried to fulfil their new roles by working even harder in the same way they have worked in the past.

It has also been interpreted as an opportunity to reduce the number of people working in the organization, resulting in some cases in 'corporate anorexia', where they have slimmed down to a level that reduces their effectiveness. Further, the systems of reward and recognition have more often than not stayed the same, with the stress on individualism and not making mistakes rather than co-operation and improvement.

I know that I have painted a particularly gloomy picture of the state of working practice today. It may not be so bad in your work situation, although I doubt if it yet matches the vision of ideal working practice suggested by the gurus.

I feel it is important to acknowledge the current reality where, to some degree, most organizations are caught between the two paradigms – traditional working practice and that of the 21st century – because as a manager you will be feeling the effects of the conflict.

# the effect on managers

Every manager wants to be successful – and recognized as such – in his or her role. How to achieve that recognition is very confused in most organizations at present.

Many of you will have been trained, formally or informally, to manage by controlling and directing. This is traditional management, where you are held responsible for everything that happens in your area and your job is to make sure that it is right. So you keep a close eye on what is going on and most important decisions are referred to you.

Even if this is your preferred style as a manager, you are likely to be finding it hard to maintain. As your responsibilities increase, due to the reduction of levels of management, the workload becomes impossible. At the same time, there are increasingly expectations that you will delegate responsibility, coach your staff, and ensure that there is continuous improvement. This is more than it is humanly possible to achieve. What's worse, if you really do change your style of management, what will be left for you to do? If you hand over responsibility and decision-making to your staff, you could be making yourself redundant, as some managers know to their cost.

Some of you will be attempting to manage in a different way. You have read the books or been on the training programmes which say that you need to lead rather than manage, and are beginning to coach your staff and empower them to make decisions. However, you are also likely to be finding it difficult:

- You may be finding that you are still held responsible for what happens and blamed if anything goes wrong, or are given policies to implement which run counter to the working practice you are trying to use.
- You may find that your staff resist the change and still ask you to make the final decisions, or want you to tell them what to do, or just won't be empowered.
- You may have found the idea of being a leader exciting, but you haven't been trained in how to make the transition, and you don't really know what to do to make the difference.

Any of these may keep pushing you back into the old role of manager, despite your good intentions. It is hard to be a manager in this time of major transition, particularly when managerial grades are disappearing with flatter organizational structures, and you are left wondering what to do to ensure you continue to have a valued role.

There is no doubt that we are headed for a radical change in the nature of management. The problem is how to develop yourself to match future requirements while still managing the current reality. It is all very well for the theorists – they don't have to deal with what is happening now.

What I want to do is to offer you some practical actions and ideas that may help you to affirm your place as a valued member of the organization. You will find that this book offers you a process for developing your skills and qualities as a 21st century manager. By going through it chapter by chapter, you will gradually add to your awareness and ability. Some will seem obvious to you, other parts may offer you a different perspective to explore. All of it is designed to give you some practical ideas on how to prepare yourself for work in the 21st century.

# the **manager as leader**

Before we can tackle how you develop the skills and qualities that will differentiate the 21st century manager, we need to define the ideal we are aiming for. After all, how will you know if you've got there if you don't know what 'there' is like?

When I explore this subject with groups of managers, I discover that, despite starting from very different views of the current reality, they do tend to have very similar views of the ideal. I am fascinated by the apparent gap between accepted practice in the workplace and the universally agreed view of what best practice is. It is as if there has been some tacit conspiracy to deny our common sense when we go into work, and to accept that you don't manage in the way that common sense dictates. Instead you manage in ways that others have managed you.

When managers *are* using their common sense, they tend to keep quiet about it, rather than broadcast their good practice. 'Don't tell anyone, but what I *really* do is . . .' is a phrase I have frequently heard, usually linked to examples of the type of management that is most effective!

*How often do you use your common sense in your work, and how often do you get caught in the trap of doing what you think managers ought to do?*

## how will it be different?

We are not talking about something completely new and alien. Effective management has always existed, if only in isolated pockets. Some managers have always recognized that they could make the most difference by managing their people in a way that released their potential rather than subduing it.

What makes this time different is that the changing workplace context is forcing managers to reconsider their role and to accept that effective people management is the only way forward, rather than a possibility if you feel courageous enough to go against the norm.

It could be described as common sense finally prevailing.

# where does it come from?

The 'new' version of management is not something that has been dreamed up by academics in their ivory towers. It is the accumulated wisdom of people observing what works best in achieving results over the long term.

## the history of management

The old-style 'command and control' management was believed to be effective when first introduced. It came directly from feudalism into industrialism and was based on a set of beliefs about the working classes that originated in the agrarian age: that they were ignorant, lazy and needed to be pushed and directed if they were to produce anything. There was little respect for the abilities and talents of the employee, and autocratic management came naturally to those first industrial managers – it was how they had always managed those who worked for them.

Not only was it natural for them to behave like this, it was also what the workers expected. They responded to it with acceptance that this was how it had to be, because they also knew that bosses treated you like this. However, there was a little more room for manoeuvre when most workers worked in agriculture, because dealing with nature imposed some limits on what could be demanded. Nature works in seasons, with natural cycles, and sets its own pace. Now, with the industrial age, there was no such limit. People were forced to work at the same pace regardless of the weather or the seasons.

It is worth noting that there were some employers who realized that ill-treatment of people is not the way to get the best work out of them. For example, the Quaker employers such as Cadbury's believed that you needed to show some care for employees. They made sure their workers were housed adequately and offered welfare facilities, canteens and so on, looking after their employees' health and well being, albeit in a somewhat paternalistic way. This tradition has been carried forward into the late 20th century, where organizations have felt that they have done enough if they have given their employees good remuneration and benefit packages, while maintaining a style of management that more closely resembles the autocratic landowners of the agrarian age. This is part of the clash between the two paradigms of management.

The over-riding method of getting people to work in the unnatural system of industrialism was by force, threat and control. Short term it was no doubt effective; longer-term, however, it resulted in trade unions to represent the right of workers to fair treatment, and a gradual revision of the view of good management and practice. It became obvious that when people are put under pressure to perform, you may squeeze a better performance out of them for a short while, but in a longer-term perspective the results deteriorate, as people rebel overtly or unconsciously against such pressure.

So the concept of a different form of management, which is more respectful of human potential, began to develop and to be applied by some of the more enlightened organizations. Yet command and control style of management continued to be the most common practice, despite evidence that it was not effective in the long term. The way most managers learned how to manage was by observing what their managers did, so the style was passed down through generations of managers.

What is more, the pressures on business continued to be short term: to reach this target of production by the end of the month, to make this much profit by the end of the quarter. To achieve short-term goals is likely to require putting pressure on employees. So the traditional practice of management has been maintained, despite the evidence that it does not pay off long term.

## why should it change now?

I have already suggested in the Introduction that we are moving into a radical transformation of the workplace. It is no longer possible to stay competitive by imposing short-term measures that show a lack of respect for employees. The people in an organization, and their motivation and commitment, are now the major factor in finding a competitive edge. The way your employees are treated is reflected in the way they treat customers and the degree to which they are motivated and innovative in their approach, and these are the factors that will differentiate your organization.

# so what are the skills and qualities of an effective manager?

I am not going to claim the credit for knowing the answer to this. As I said before, many have explored this subject and what they come up with is remarkably similar. What I will do is offer you a summary of the main characteristics highlighted by those who have researched the subject, and by managers examining their own ideal.

## 1 a role model for employees

This is all-encompassing and is significant when we look at developing the qualities required. It recognizes that people take more notice of what you do than of what you tell them to do. It means that managers have to practise what they preach, in their everyday behaviour, and set a clear example of an effective and committed worker.

> Richard Branson was being interviewed. He said that he dressed informally and fooled around to encourage his staff to do the same. He wanted them to see fun as an essential element of work, rather than something that only happened in your personal life. He felt that if he approached work with a sense of fun, he would help to influence others to do the same.

In one sense, being the model is a major responsibility because it means accepting that how you are has the greatest influence on how others are. Yet this is factual, it is what happens, so its acceptance relieves you, as manager, of the difficulty of trying to get others to behave in a way which for you would be uncomfortable.

## 2 self-aware

Stephen Covey describes this as working from the inside out. It implies that managers continue to explore ways of managing themselves effectively before trying to manage others.

They recognize their own strengths and weaknesses, have control over their moods, know how to bring out the best in themselves. Clearly this is vital if you are to be the model for others.

A manager told me that his major personal issue was his intolerance when others didn't catch on to the ideas he was putting forward. He saw them as stupid, and knew that it wasn't useful, or even accurate. We worked on how he could change this attitude to something more useful, while recognizing that his enthusiasm for making a difference was a very positive attribute.

## 3 a learner

It is essential that managers recognize and acknowledge that they are continually learning and developing. Many managers feel that they have to pretend to know it all or they will lose face. In the rapidly changing world we live in, it is those who are open to different ideas, who are always looking for the opportunity to learn and develop, who will thrive.

What is more, this is an essential part of the model they provide. We have all been taught to try and get things right, rather than be innovative and experimental. Only if managers are willing to 'seek out surprises, relish the unpredictable', as Margaret Wheatley puts it, will staff become comfortable with doing the same. What is more, only those who are still learning can develop self-awareness.

One of Jane's team came to her with a problem in the manufacturing process. Jane had never come across this problem before either. She declared that she didn't know what to do, and suggested that they both went and looked at it to see if they could work it out. She suggested they might need an engineer to help as well. Her team member then said that he had an idea about what to do, but had been afraid to try it, in case it was wrong. 'Let's try it!' said Jane.

Her team member talked about that incident for months afterwards, because it had really made him realize that she meant it when she said that they all had to learn and develop together.

## 4 delighting in change

The effective manager has learned to work with change rather than resist it. He or she recognizes that change is likely to be the only constant in the future, and enjoys the challenge and potential for learning which that entails. As Tom Peters suggests, 'Leadership is learning to love change.'

When there are no obvious signs of external pressure for change, the effective manager will still look for ways of creating change, by challenging conventional wisdom and asking 'What else?' and 'How else?' This links to being a learner, because change and difference are the keys for learning to occur.

I remember when I worked in adult education, my boss was constantly looking for ways of changing, in every sense. He would ask if we could think of new courses to offer, and come up with outrageous ideas himself. He was always asking how we could improve processes like recruitment, enrolment and registration, what would improve the atmosphere of the centre, and what else we could do to make learning an enjoyable experience. Some people hated working for him, because he didn't allow us to settle into a routine. I loved knowing that I could suggest something out of the ordinary and he would enthusiastically encourage me and help me make it work.

## 5  a visionary

For change to be effective, there needs to be a framework for the delight in change. Having a clear vision of where you are going provides this framework. If the manager does not have an ideal picture in his or her head of how the working practice can be, what the organization can achieve, how people will work more effectively, then there is no direction to any developments and no way of telling if they are useful or not.

Three years ago, a departmental manager in a financial services organization envisaged his department being a model of new working practice. Everyone told him it was impossible: the organization as a whole was hierarchical and traditional and most of his staff had been there for years and were stuck in their ways.

He didn't agree that it was impossible and held to his vision, gradually shifting the ground and accepting that sometimes there were setbacks. His department is now well on its way to being that model.

## 6  full awareness of current reality

This characteristic needs to be linked to the previous one of being a visionary. I call it having double vision! To successfully work towards an ideal, you need to be very clear about where you are now. So often, managers claim that everything is fine until some crisis occurs which reveals the flaws. This is linked to not losing face – it is not yet accepted practice to say, 'I haven't succeeded in making that work yet.'

It is the tension between current reality and the ideal that can produce the active development. Peter Senge calls the gap 'creative tension' and suggests that it is useful when it leads to positive change to move closer to the vision. It is not helpful to perceive the gap as a reason to lower your goals – this leads to a continuing regression, instead of progress.

> The departmental manager referred to in the previous example wanted his senior management team to delegate responsibility to their teams and become leaders. Two embraced the concept with enthusiasm, two refused point blank, coming up with cogent reasons to maintain their existing control.
>
> He accepted that he couldn't force them, and allowed them to continue for a while, gradually experimenting with ways of tempting them into changing their style. He still does not claim to have fully succeeded, and he's still working on it.

## 7  ethics and values

To use current reality as a force for positive creative tension, rather than a reason to give up or to try and bully people into movement (old-style management to try to achieve a new working practice!) it is essential that the manager has clarified for him- or herself a high standard of ethics and values. Commentators such as Rosabeth Moss Kanter and Stephen Covey stress the importance of this as the driving force for shaping the approach to leadership, and every checklist of qualities and skills of leadership ever produced in groups I have run features words like 'has integrity' and 'ethical'.

The Body Shop's founder, Anita Roddick, has from the beginning insisted on cruelty-free products. She also makes sure that the Body Shop engages with Third World producers in fair and ethical trade. What is more, the Body Shop supports national and international causes for justice, fair trade, etc. The staff have a charter which ensures that they are treated fairly, and all of them engage in community service as part of their contract. Not only does the ethical stance show through in the Body Shop's external image, it also is evident in the way staff are treated within the company.

## 8  systemic thinking

As well as having a strong value system, the leader has to develop a different way of thinking. Systemic thinking means being aware of how processes work, and separating causes from symptoms. Deming suggested that the majority of work problems are caused by systems, not people – people's behaviour is merely the symptom of a systemic cause.

This way of thinking has two major effects: it removes the blame culture and it gives a longer-term perspective. Peter Senge gives a clear pragmatic description of systemic thinking in *The Fifth Discipline*, and reminds us that the idea that cause and effect is a straight-line relationship has rarely proved to be the case.

A training officer in a major retail company complained that she was being blocked in doing her job. When we explored the issue we discovered that there was no clear accepted role definition. She was clear what her job was, but others saw it quite differently, and there was no objective description to refer to. The solution was to clarify her role with her line manager and to have an agreed description she could use to support her attempts to introduce new development work. The problem was not that others were being deliberately obstructive to her, it was that her line manager had given her a different role to the previous occupant, and no one else in the organization knew it.

## 9 communicating well

A manager could have all the qualities listed above and still fall down on the ideal if he or she were unable to communicate clearly with others. This doesn't mean giving slick presentations, it means being able to build relationships with others and to convey your message clearly and congruently. It is being able to express things clearly and simply in ways that others can understand, and showing genuine interest or concern. If said with feeling the message gets through, even if you are not terribly accurate.

> I remember a youth worker in a community centre where I used to work who was a very proper public school type – a real English gentleman. He always had waiting lists for his mountaineering weekends, and I wondered why the kids related so well to him – they seemed worlds apart, this man with his posh education, and the kids from an inner-city area. I decided to go on one of his weekends and find out.
>
> When we had all fought our way to the top of the mountain, with him encouraging and bullying us all the way, he just stood there and swore profusely, waving his arms around. The lad next to him turned to me and said, 'He's right, isn't he? This is f***ing wonderful and worth the pain! It reminds us that Birmingham isn't all there is in the world.'

## 10 thinking positively

It is important that the leader has a positive view of things. It is all too easy to get caught in the mire of negative thinking, so that problems and obstacles seem to be all there is, particularly since that seems to be a prevalent way of thinking in our Western cultures.

The leader looks at what's possible, rather than the constraints. He or she believes that things can change for the better, and finds ways of making it happen. He or she also tends to have a sense of humour, which helps to keep things in perspective when they don't go according to plan.

A friend of mine was made redundant. Rather than see it as an indictment of her abilities and value, she saw it as an opportunity to look for an employer who would really value her and stretch her capabilities further. I asked her what she would miss from her old job. 'The lousy food in the canteen,' she replied. 'In fact, it will be one of my criteria for my next job: the food in the staff canteen has to be good!'

A month later, she started a new job with more responsibility and more autonomy. I rang to congratulate her. 'This is just what I wanted,' she said, 'but then, life tends to work out doesn't it!'

## 11 enthusiasm

I think this quality deserves a section to itself, because it underlies a lot of the other characteristics. The word 'enthusiastic' originally meant 'having God within'. It is an endearing and infectious characteristic, and carries people through situations successfully even if they haven't quite got other things just so. It implies a genuine belief in what you're doing or saying, and a genuine will to make it successful.

Children have this quality in almost everything they do, until they learn to control it. It is natural and preferable to be able to enter into something heart and soul, rather than just go through the motions. And that enthusiasm engages others at an emotional level rather than just an intellectual level, which is essential if you are really going to make a difference.

I remember going to see Bruce Springsteen at an open-air concert. At first, most of the audience just stood still and watched and listened. They were conveying the usual British 'detachment'.

Springsteen was obviously thoroughly enjoying himself. He put his heart and soul into his performance, singing, dancing, telling stories, laughing with pure pleasure. By the end of the concert, three hours later, almost everyone in the audience was singing along, laughing, clapping, dancing. His enthusiasm was infectious.

## 12 being real

The characteristics I've listed so far are all skills or qualities we can develop and work on. This final one is what we are already! I often call it being human, because it's the recognition that none of us is perfect, and we all have a unique individual permutation of qualities that make us who we are.

One person is loud and jolly, another quiet and calm, some people like to be up front, others lead while staying in the background. We all have times when we don't know what to do, times when we're sure. It is much more comfortable to be around someone who is as human as we are in these situations, than to be with someone who puts on a front.

John Harvey-Jones, ex-chairman of ICI, is a well-respected and well-liked business consultant and speaker. Ask people what they like about him, and they are almost certain to include comments on his unruly hair, his outrageous ties and his down-to-earth manner of speaking. It is his unique personality that comes across. He is not some bland PR creation – he's real.

## the impossible dream?

As you read through this checklist of the characteristics of the ideal leader, did you find yourself making unfavourable comparisons between yourself and this ideal?

The list can look daunting, leaving us asking, 'How can I possibly attain this ideal?' Yet many have achieved it, in many different walks of life. There have been business managers, community leaders, even politicians, who have displayed this combination of characteristics and proved their effectiveness. It is from these exemplars that the ideal has developed.

They didn't all start out already fully developed. Most of them started with a few of the characteristics and then developed those further, and the others to complement them. Look again at the list:

1. A role model for employees.
2. Self-aware.
3. A learner.

4. Delighting in change.
5. A visionary.
6. Full awareness of current reality.
7. Ethics and values.
8. Systemic thinking.
9. Communicating well.
10. Thinking positively.
11. Enthusiasm.
12. Being real.

*Notice how many of these characteristics you do have, at least to some degree. Maybe you tend to show them in contexts other than work – at home, or socially – but they do exist in your personality. List examples of where you use these characteristics already.*

You will notice that the list doesn't mention things like empowering others and delegating responsibility. This is because they are the resultant actions of the ideal manager, rather than the characteristics. The behaviours that demonstrate these characteristics are dealt with later in the book.

You need to recognize that you are not starting from scratch, and that it is possible to build on what you already have. In the next chapter we will begin to explore where you start with that building, and how you can do it.

# believing **that effective management works**

It is all very well defining the characteristics of an excellent leader, but before we will really commit to developing ourselves to match that picture, we have to be convinced that we can be effective in this redefined role. As people say to me, 'It's a great ideal, but I live in the real world.'

So how do we make the shift from cynicism to conviction? The intellectual shift happens as we receive more and more information telling us that it's important. But the most important shift is in our emotions: when we feel that it's right, we are more likely to move beyond lip service into real practice.

## the process for shifting our beliefs and attitudes

If we are to genuinely change our behaviour as managers, we need to first shift our beliefs and attitudes. They drive our behaviour, and it is those we're unconsciously holding on to that are preventing us from making the emotional shift.

### what are my beliefs about management?

In Chapters 1 and 2 I discussed where these beliefs about management come from, and the first stage is to become aware of them. The 'real world' referred to earlier is the work environment which is run on the basis of these traditional beliefs.

# what is the ideal of the effective manager?

In Chapter 2 I suggested that there is a commonly held view of the ideal, and spelt it out in some detail. We need this clear picture of what we are aiming at so that we can notice where our beliefs and values do and do not fit with the ideal.

*As you read through the checklist of ideal characteristics of the 21st century manager, did you find that there were some that you disagreed with, or that made you think, 'That will never work in my organization.' Notice where you have some beliefs that may need shifting.*

# why should I move?

If we are to begin to deal with our emotional reactions to shifting beliefs, we have to give ourselves a good reason to do so. These reasons are not a carefully thought out rational argument. That is only going to work on an intellectual level. We may say, 'I can understand that it's important' as a result of such argument, but that does not commit us to action.

We are essentially selfish creatures, and we make changes when we can see some pay-off for ourselves. What we think these pay-offs will be will vary according to our own values and the particular context we work in. It is not possible to produce a definitive list, but it is possible to produce your own customized list, and that is the first stage of convincing yourself.

*Reconsider the characteristics of an ideal 21st century manager. What do you think the pay-offs would be for you in becoming this ideal? List as many as you can think of. (An example of such a list, produced by a group of managers, is given at the end of the chapter for comparison.)*

These potential pay-offs for you personally are the reasons why it would be worth your while to begin the development.

# how do I know it will work?

At this stage, some of those beliefs we hold about what's possible switch in. We find ourselves doubting whether it is really likely to be possible to get these pay-offs from practising the ideal. After all, we have lots of evidence already collected that makes us think that you have to manage the way we do now. Will the changes really bring the benefits we would like?

To counteract these doubts, we need to find evidence to support the notion that being a 21st century manager will bring the pay-offs we want. The best way to do this is to think of examples of people who are displaying the characteristics and gaining similar pay-offs to the ones we want. You will have noticed as you went through Chapter 2 that I gave an example of someone displaying each characteristic as I listed them. Some were examples from my own experience, some were taken from books or articles I've read about the person concerned, or interviews with them. These people are all benefiting in ways I want to from being leaders. When I explore more to find out how they feel they're gaining from the style of leadership they have, I discover that there are other gains which I hadn't thought of, so I can add them to my list of pay-offs.

> I asked a managing director I know why he had changed his style to that of a leader. He said his original reasons were that he thought it would make his life easier, and he would be able to hand over responsibility and have more time for himself. Once he had begun the process, he found that there were far more gains than he thought. He now thoroughly enjoyed going to work, he had learned an enormous amount from his staff, and he had a much more appreciative and constructive relationship with all his employees.

*Think of some examples of people who are displaying the characteristics of a leader and gaining from it. Come up with at least eight examples. (If you find this difficult, ask colleagues to join in with their examples, or read some of the books on the reading list at the end of this book.) Don't forget to add any extra gains to your pay-off list.*

## can I do this?

Once we have given ourselves more evidence that being a 21st century manager does have the pay-offs we want, we are left with nagging self-doubt. Others may be able to pull it off, but am I capable of doing the same?

The fear that we may not be capable of fulfilling this role of the 21st century manager can be very powerful, although it would rarely be acknowledged openly. If you are already a manager, then the last thing you want to do is to risk a different approach and fail. This would be putting your job on the line, and while you are getting by as you are, it is hard to take a risk.

So we need a lot of reassurance that being this type of manager is within our capability and will not make us look foolish. This requires a review of our experience, to find clear examples of being able to fulfil the role.

## reluctance to acknowledge our abilities

Acknowledging what we can do sounds easy, but it isn't for most of us. We have been brought up in a culture that values modesty and self-effacement. We are told from an early age not to boast, so we learn to play down our achievements. What is more, if you do claim to be good at something, you get the feeling that everyone is waiting to catch you out.

> I remember being surprised and hurt as a young child when my new form teacher asked me to spell 'cataclysmic', and I spelt it with an 'i' instead of a 'y'. She triumphantly announced: 'I thought you were supposed to be brilliant at spelling, but you got that wrong!' I was 9, I hadn't heard or seen the word before, and I didn't think I'd done too badly! The experience made me very cautious about acknowledging that I was good at spelling, and I wished that the headmaster wouldn't tell people that I was clever.

So we learn to be wary of saying that we're good at something, or right about something, unless we're 110 per cent certain that we won't get caught out by someone finding a counter-example. We even give the counter-examples ourselves, to stop others from doing it.

> I commented that I was impressed by the way a manager had handled a difficult session with a member of staff. She immediately said, 'Yes, but I could have defused the situation before it started, and I didn't handle John so well last week.'

As you begin to look for examples of yourself demonstrating the characteristics of a leader, you will find that 'yes, buts' come up for you too. In order to counteract them, you need to acknowledge to yourself that the examples you find may not be perfect examples, but they are indicators that you have the capability to be a 21st century manager.

You are not expected to be fully formed and perfect as a 21st century manager – in fact, one of the major characteristics is being a learner, being in the process of developing further.

*Look again at the list of characteristics of a 21st century leader. Take each one in turn and identify a couple of times when you have demonstrated the characteristic. It may have been in your work situation; it may have been in your personal life. It doesn't matter which, as we are merely looking for examples of having the capability. Here are some examples:*

- *I am very real when I am on holiday with my friends.*
- *I use systemic thinking in relation to my garden.*
- *I was a visionary when I began to explore the use of computers at work 15 years ago.*

As you begin to undertake this exercise, you will find that more and more examples come to mind. You will have more examples in some categories than others. That's OK. We all start from a slightly different baseline, depending on our experience and existing strengths. What matters is that you identify that you do have a baseline to start from.

# how do I start?

Once you have worked through the process of tackling the beliefs you hold which restrict you, and the doubts about the viability of the development for you, then you are ready to begin the process of developing yourself to be that 21st century leader.

At this point, it is easy to get stuck again. There aren't many guides to this form of development, either as written or recorded texts, or as live models and examples. Those that do exist seem to assume that you have nothing else to do while you engage in this development.

The reality is that you are already up to your ears in work and life, and you don't have the time or energy to pursue this single-mindedly. If you are going to undertake this development, there are three requirements to be met:

1.  To be manageable within your existing everyday life. You need a series of small steps you can take which will only require small chunks of time, so that you can set yourself something to 'do' each week and feel that it is achievable.
2.  To feel safe to undertake it within your current working reality. A few unusual individuals take great leaps of faith into a different working practice. Most of us prefer not to rock the boat too much, either individually or organizationally. We want to feel that our development takes account of the context within which we are working, both personally and professionally.

3. To give some positive gains quickly. When we are undertaking something new, we are encouraged to continue if there is some obvious gain fairly early on.

It is with these requirements in mind that I have planned the rest of this book. If you follow it through in order, you will find that it offers you ways of meeting these requirements, at the same time building up your ability and practice as a 21st century leader.

# where do I start?

The good news is that you have already started! If you have come this far through the book and done the activities I've suggested, then you have already laid the foundation of self-development. The way we think about things is a crucial aspect of our potential for development. If you are now wanting to take this potential on to the next stage, then you have already made it easier for yourself to do so.

# conclusion

In this chapter we have examined the process of developing belief in our ability to be a 21st century manager. I have dealt with the questions that arise in our minds when we consider starting any form of development:

- What exactly am I aiming for; what is the ideal?
- Why should I bother; what will I gain?
- How do I know it will work?
- Can I do it?
- How do I start?

This process can be used whenever we need to make some change or development. It gives us a useful mind-set for entering the development proper, and enables us to approach the change with a positive attitude.

# potential pay-offs for becoming an excellent leader

My company has an edge
Fulfilment
Peace
Quiet influence
Make things better
Less hassles
Success for others
Other people work hard for my vision
Female in a male-dominated environment
More interesting things to choose to do
We'll sell more – long term
Recognition
Promotion
Development opportunity
Power
Improved team performance
More comfortable life
*Want* to go to work
Being seen to achieve results
Happy customers
Having less interpersonal conflict to deal with

Feel good
Integrity
I get to learn more
Earn more
Kudos
Make a difference
More choices
I get to laugh/smile more
People want me to help
Joy from feeling others growing
Satisfaction
Rewards – money and status
Reduce pressure/stress
Sense of achievement
More pay
Respect
Happy team
Being liked
Warm feeling
Delight
Quality service and product
Developing people who do not see themselves as important or who do not think they need to and cannot/will not look forward

# endpiece

## and if it's hard to accept this view of the context

As someone said to me recently, there is a lot of evidence that behaving as we have always behaved works and is acceptable – even preferable – within our organizations. We all know that technology has changed some things, but it is not yet clear that it means we *have to* manage in a different way.

If you find yourself rehearsing the reasons why you don't need to develop yourself more as a people manager, then I suggest you do two or three things to help you make sense of the changes that are taking place.

1.  *Read:* choose from the suggested reading list books that appeal to you, whether those on theory or those that are biographical, and extend your views of what is happening and what is likely to happen.
2.  *Look for examples of 'new' management:* you may find these in organizations – living case studies – or in magazines. Notice the effectiveness of 'new' managers and how much they enjoy their jobs, and remind yourself that you are as capable as they are of changing style.
3.  *Remind yourself of the benefits of making a change in your style:* read through again the possible benefits of changing your approach to management. If you are not convinced that it is a necessity, work on the basis that it could be worth it anyway in terms of the results for you and your staff.

# Part II

# Transforming Yourself

This section of the book concentrates on how we develop the characteristics we require as leaders, and how we apply them to our working practice.

The emphasis is on self-development, rather than doing things to those you lead. We need to be able to set an example to others before we try to affect their behaviour in any other way. This is often called 'walking the talk'.

In Part II you can pick and choose which areas you feel will be most useful to you, if you want to. There is a natural progression in the order of the chapters, but you may find that some of them are aspects you already feel are well developed, and you can just use them to reaffirm your strengths. Others you may spend more time on and use to develop areas you are less sure of.

Do remember that these aspects of transforming yourself are not alien to you. What I am offering you are reminders of best practice and simple ways of using your common sense more effectively.

It is the cumulative effect of enhanced practice that creates the 21st century manager.

# dealing **with** **change**

Before we can really work on developing our skills and qualities to be excellent 21st century managers, we need to ensure that we are fully aware of the context we are working in and the level of change that is occurring.

Unless it feels urgent and important, we will not put this development high up on our list of priorities. In order to bring the subject to the fore, we have to confront our attitudes to change and our habitual views of how things happen.

## what do we mean by change?

Traditionally, we have seen change as something you had to do in order to find a new place to stop. If we changed jobs, we then re-established a routine in the new job, so that it was familiar and habitual. If we changed a process or structure in the organization, then we learned the new one and settled down again.

Change has been seen as an occasional necessary evil, which created a period of turmoil before we could settle back into routine again. This view no longer applies. Change is the only thing that is predictable in future working practice.

Alvin Toffler, writing in the late 1960s, predicted what he called 'The Third Wave': a post-industrial society with an accelerated rate of change, such that any adaptations to the situation would be temporary, as the next change would already be on its way. At that time, he was out on a limb with his predictions. Most of us had not had experiences that suggested to us that he knew what he was talking about. Now Toffler is a well-respected consultant for the US government on adapting for the future.

The only way to deal with the accelerated rate of change is to be a change agent, to take a proactive role rather than to look for some place to stop.

## is there really accelerated change?

Toffler described the chain reaction of change as:

*Discovery* → *Application* → *Impact* → *Diffusion*

The span of time between discovery and diffusion – that is, it becoming commonplace in society – has been dramatically reducing over the past century.

Within our adult lives, computers have become commonplace; VCRs are a normal piece of household equipment; large numbers of people use credit or debit cards for shopping; products are made by automation; and the number of cars owned has multiplied exponentially. This is just for starters!

> I remember when automated bank tills were first introduced – and I'm not that old! They seemed very 'hi-tech' to me, and I was afraid to use them, preferring to run to the bank in my lunch-hour to do my transactions. Now I can't imagine managing my finances without the 'hole in the wall', not to mention the telephone banking service I now use which is 24 hours a day, seven days a week.

*Use your own experience to prove this to yourself. Look at some of the technology we take for granted. Think for a moment or two about the changes that have happened since the 1960s, 1970s and 1980s. Notice how much more quickly they become commonplace and accepted. What do you now use regularly that wasn't a possibility for your parents, or even for you when you were younger?*

## where is it leading?

When you hear someone like Bill Gates, head of Microsoft Corporation, talk about technology, you realize that we have hardly begun to experience the impact of technological change on our everyday domestic and working lives. It is already possible to replicate any product within weeks of its appearance. The speed of communications, through computer networks, faxes and phones, combined with the ability to technically 'reverse engineer' a product – work backwards through the process of creating it – mean that anything can be cloned worldwide in no time at all. What comes next we can only guess at.

I remember seeing an in-company video a couple of years ago, about likely developments in computer and communications technology in the next decade. I thought it was rather far-fetched, with a science-fiction feel to it. When I made this comment to the person sitting next to me, he laughed at me and said that they already had the technology to do all of this and more. They were at the stage of making it commercially viable and socially acceptable. 'Commercially viable is not difficult,' he said. 'It's persuading people to accept this type of impact on their normal lives which is hard.'

# accepting change as the norm

Once we have stopped and recognized the role of change now occurring in our society, we need to consciously make a shift in our beliefs about change. You remember I suggested that 'change' has tended to be seen as a necessary evil before the next stopping place. This becomes untenable when change is constant and ever-accelerating.

## filtering for change

We need to re-educate ourselves so that change is seen as the norm rather than the exception. Part of that re-education happens as soon as we stop and consider all the changes that are taking place in our world now, as we did in the last section.

Our conscious minds can only hold limited amounts of information at a time, although our unconscious stores much, much more. The way we choose what to be aware of consciously is through our beliefs. If I believe the world is a cruel place, then I will notice all the instances of cruelty that support this belief. If I believe the world is a kind place, I will notice all the instances of kindness to support that. (This explains why two people with contradictory beliefs are equally certain that they are right – they have been amassing evidence to prove their own belief and ignoring any contradictory evidence.)

So if we are to believe that change is the norm, we have to consciously choose to collect evidence to support that belief.

---

When I think about changes in my own life, I realize that they're never-ending. I have a different hairstyle from a year ago; I work for several different companies to a year ago; my diet has changed significantly; I walk much more than I used to; my son no longer lives with me; my partner is also my business development manager; I have more wrinkles – the list goes on and on, with a mixture of trivial and life-changing differences.

---

*We have already stopped to consider changes in the world. Now stop and think about changes in your own life: moving jobs and homes, changing habits, differences in working practice, even physical and emotional changes you have experienced. How many can you identify in 10 minutes? List them on a piece of paper.*

## viewing change as a positive force

Once we have composed this initial list, we can use it to help us to revise our view of change. While we believed that change was a necessary evil, we would tend to notice the negative effects of change, rather than the positive effects. So we would comment on the disruptions, the uncertainty, the need to learn new things, rather than the positives. Yet most changes have a positive effect as well. Sometimes we need to take a longer term view to notice this.

For example, moving house is disruptive, but when I look back at my last move, I can see how it made me sort out my stuff and clear the rubbish out, how much more pleasant my environment is now, and how much I found out about how others live by visiting so many houses!

*Take your list of changes you have experienced and consider each one in turn. What were the positives you got out of each of these changes? Find some, even if your normal reaction would be negative. For example:*

*Getting more wrinkles: I like the signs of being older and wiser, and they express my character more.*
*My diet has changed significantly: I'm healthier.*

They say that we get what we expect. If we choose to expect change to bring us some form of benefit, then we are more likely to find those benefits.

## change as room for manoeuvre

The third aspect of change which we can reconsider is the way it removes taken-for-granteds. When change is happening, everything is in a state of flux. It is the ideal opportunity to make other changes you know will be useful to you.

> When the company was restructured, Joan was told that her role was to be redefined. She saw this as an opportunity to move from being a glorified secretary to making her job more interesting and responsible. She asked her line manager if she could make some suggestions to contribute to the discussion about her role.
>
> Her line manager was a little wary, but agreed to discuss her ideas. When he saw that she was more than willing to take on extra responsibility, he was delighted. It led to him agreeing that it would be more efficient if everyone word processed their own letters, memos and notes, instead of hand writing them and giving them to Joan to process.

The 'rules' that are set in concrete about how things are done become loosened when there is change. There is space to make change work for you.

*Think of a change at work that potentially gave you more room for manoeuvre. Did you take advantage of it?*

## imposed change and chosen change

There are differences between changes that are imposed on us and changes that we choose to make. We would all prefer to have only chosen change in our life, because then we feel in control of the situation. However, none of us is in that privileged position. We are affected by global changes even if we control most of the changes in our lives, and for most of us the work environment will include a lot of imposed changes.

It is important to recognize that we need to feel some sense of control in change situations, and that means becoming a change agent – being active in change situations rather than simply reacting to them.

## reaction to change

The normal reaction to change is to resist. There are lots of ways in which we may do this, for example:

- say no;
- think of reasons why it won't work;
- be very slow and clumsy in implementing it;
- only do the bare minimum and otherwise carry on as you were;
- do what's required, but with no enthusiasm or initiative.

This explains why so many change programmes in the workplace don't have the desired effect. If these forms of resistance are not dealt with, they subvert the process and people carry on with previous ways of doing things.

## dealing with resistance

So what can we do about this reaction? First we need to recognize that it is what happens in most cases. Then we need to give space for it, as part of the process of change. You cannot force people to change without increasing resistance and reducing their morale. By allowing for their resistance and letting them express their fears, concerns and regrets, you can ease them past this phase of the process.

- *Allow space for regret.* Let people talk about what they will miss from the old way. (This often shows that some of what they think they will miss will in fact be part of the new way as well.)
- *Identify what you have gained from the old way that will continue to be useful to you.* Encourage people to notice that there is some continuity, that the new always builds on the old in some ways.
- *Discuss what you will be glad to get rid of.* Encourage people to notice the aspects of the old way that they won't miss. (This helps to broaden their perspective and remind them that the 'old days' are not all golden.)
- *Look at fears and concerns about the change.* Allow people to express their fears and concerns. (This gives you information about what you need to cater for as the change is implemented.)

■ *Ask people what benefits they think there will be from the change.* Encourage them to identify positive gains from the change. (This starts to move their frame of mind.)

By allowing for this process you reduce the resistance. It is similar to the process of bereavement. Unless you have time to let go of the past and go through the feelings associated with it, you cannot move forward easily.

---

A group of employees in a major manufacturing company were up in arms at an imposed change in team structures. I had worked with them before, and was asked if I could help. I started the session by asking them what they would miss about the old way. The manager tried to stop me, saying that it would only make things worse – they were already negative and didn't need any more reasons to stay like that. I asked him to let it run, and he reluctantly agreed.

As we moved to the second part of the process, the atmosphere began to change. People laughed and joked about some of the bad aspects of how it was. Their fears and concerns turned out to be mostly about not being capable of fulfilling the new demands – something the manager could immediately reassure them about – and when it came to possible benefits, they became cautiously optimistic. The real process of change had begun, and the manager began to breathe more easily.

---

*Think of an imposed change in your working life, and go through this process for yourself. Notice how this structures your thoughts and feelings about the situation into a form that is useful. We can use this process for ourselves first to help ourselves to begin to re-think our attitudes towards change, and then of course we can use it to help others to become more positive in times of change.*

## influencing change

The advantage of change creating a space in the accepted practice is that you can use it to move beyond normal reactions to change.

We can become proactive in helping to bring out the potential positive effects of change. We can enter into changes with the question 'How can I make this work well?' instead of the resistant question 'Why do we have to change?' Then we set our mind-frame to ensuring that the potential benefits of the change are brought about.

Most organizational changes create unforeseen gaps or needs for adaptation, and are broad sweeps of the brush, rather than painting the fine detail. By becoming involved at an early stage in the process of implementation, we can influence how the gaps are filled, how the detail is completed.

A department in a financial services organization was planning major changes to its working practice. The head of department had come up with the basic vision, but wanted to involve his staff in taking it into more detail. All staff were invited to take part in workshops where the implications would be discussed and people could put forward suggestions as to how the new systems were implemented.

Almost 40 per cent of the staff joined in. Their feedback from the sessions was used to help put together the implementation plan. They reported how this process made them feel a part of the change and made them more positive about it. The pay-off, both in terms of useful ideas and staff morale was tremendous. The majority of the rest of the staff then asked if they could also have a session, because they saw how much the others had gained from the process.

By getting involved in sorting out how the change will work, we regain some control over the situation and act more as we would if it were a chosen change.

## promoting change

We learn to revise our view of change by dealing effectively with our own resistance and by noticing how we can influence what happens even when it's imposed. This leads us towards an attitude to change that is quite different: we begin to see change as a positive and important part of our experience.

This is not really something alien to us. It is a return to our childlike nature. As a child, we delighted in difference, the new, the unusual. It was what made life exciting and gave us a chance to learn and grow. Only when we listened to adults did we pick up the message that change was a difficulty rather than a delight. Some people managed to avoid getting the message!

Once change has become exciting and attractive to us again, we want it to be part of our life and we begin to actively promote change.

## what does this mean?

It means that we are not only actively influencing change when it is imposed, we are also looking for opportunities to make change happen.

My brother has run his own company for three years. Before that, he was self-employed for a while, but when that business was ticking over, he decided to employ some others to help him. First it was one, then two, then three, then four. Once he had the business thriving, after a couple of years, he began to look for the next change. So now he is busy delegating responsibility for the business to his employees, so that they will be able to set up on their own if they want to. And his question is always: 'What next?' As he says, this is what makes life exciting – it's boring if it's just ticking over nicely.

If you look around at those who seem to be doing well in our world, you will find that they are all people who thrive on change and seek out opportunities to make it happen.

*Think about your own examples of people like this: people in the public eye, or people you know personally. Notice how they delight in the new or different and how they create changes in their lives, both personally and professionally. Now notice times when you have also actively promoted change and how you felt when you did. It may be at work or in your personal life, and the changes may be big or small.*

## delighting in change

By becoming an active agent of change we are working with what is happening in the world, rather than resisting it. And it's more comfortable to 'go with the flow' than to fight it. Compare the feelings we have when we resist change to the feelings we have when we take an active part in it. It's inevitable that there will be change, constantly. It's up to us to choose to deal with that in a way that makes us feel good.

Once we begin to find change exciting rather than fearful, we can take some control of our own destiny again and decide to use the constant change to our own advantage.

# technological change

I want to pick out a specific example of change that is generally imposed and that will be more and more prevalent in business as we go forward into the next century.

Use of computers is here to stay and they will play an ever-increasing role in our lives, both at work and at home. Some people have accepted the challenge of new technology and run with it. They not only use their computers well at work, they also have them at home. They 'play' on the Internet, they use them to keep their personal accounts, they produce posters for community events, and they generally enjoy and learn from their computers.

Others are still trying to avoid the implications of technological change. They do the bare minimum required using computers, and stick to the old tried and tested ways of achieving results. These people will tell you of all the times they have seen problems caused by the use of computers rather than listing all the benefits which accrue through their use. Unfortunately, many of these 'technophobes' are managers who are often telling their staff that they must use computers! Not an example of providing a good role model or delighting in change.

*What is your position on the use of the computers? Have you learned how to use one for various purposes? Do you regularly use the Internet – and not just for e-mail? Are you planning to enhance your skills in this area? Look at where you stand now and identify how you could develop yourself even further in this area. It is vital for the 21st century manager.*

# working with others on change

What I have taken you through so far is the process of becoming a change agent, someone who handles change well and delights in change. What we are doing with this process is gradually re-educating ourselves in our beliefs, attitudes and behaviours concerning change.

Once we have worked through this process we can begin to help others to engage in the same voyage of discovery. This may seem quite risky, because it requires trusting them to be constructive and positive. And some will still resist and refuse to be convinced that change is either necessary or positive. They are, however, a small minority, in my experience. Most people want to thrive in our changing world. Their resistance is habitual rather than deliberate. Most of us were not prepared, through our upbringing and education, for a rapidly changing world and so do not know how to be change agents.

By helping people to work through the process, we make life easier, for ourselves and for them: easier for us, because we reinforce it in ourselves and reduce the amount of resistance we meet when we have to or choose to implement changes; easier for them because it is more satisfying to actively engage with change than it is to resist it.

## so what is the process of becoming a change agent?

I will summarize for you the process we have covered in this chapter:

- Becoming consciously aware of the accelerated rate of change in our society.
- Collecting evidence that change is the norm.
- Viewing change as a positive force by collecting evidence of the benefits of change.
- Recognizing that change leaves space for you to influence what happens.
- Allowing for resistance to change by following the natural path to reducing resistance:
  - express regrets about what's being left behind;
  - identify the gains to be brought forward;
  - discuss what you'll be glad to get rid of;
  - express fears and concerns about the change;
  - ask people to identify potential benefits of the change.
- Noticing how you can influence the change by becoming actively involved in the process of implementation.
- Moving to actively suggesting changes.

As a manager you may find the first five steps easier than the last two. Up to there, your work with others will make it easier for you to impose changes. In the last two steps, you are encouraging them to take some control of the situation, and even be the ones who suggest the changes.

You have to believe that your staff also have wisdom and awareness. In my experience, the suggestions made are mostly useful and show sensitivity to the context. Sometimes they challenge the status quo, but that's what this is all about, isn't it?

## conclusion

Obviously there is a lot more to be discussed on the subject of change, and others have written more extensively on this (see the reading list on p. 207 for some useful references). However, in the context of becoming a 21st century manager it is important that we recognize that we are working in a different paradigm, where change is the norm, even if resistance as per the old paradigm is also still the norm.

We need to retrain ourselves into being change agents who work with what is happening and work to make even more happen. As Tom Peters says, 'Today, loving change, tumult, even chaos is a prerequisite for survival, let alone success.'

# preparing **yourself for effective management**

Up until now we have been concerned with preparing the ground for being an effective manager in times of change. We have explored how to set up your beliefs and attitudes to support you in wanting to make the most of the opportunities that change brings. Yet, however convinced you are, whether you put it into effect or not will depend on how you are feeling at the time.

It is vital that we know how to put ourselves into a state where we can approach our role in the most constructive way. When you found examples of yourself demonstrating the characteristics of an effective manager, I can guarantee that it was at a time when you were feeling good in yourself. In this chapter we will consider ways of creating that state for yourself.

Now this may appear to be at a tangent to the main thrust of what we are looking at: you have prepared yourself to make your first steps towards development and expect to take action in your management of others. Instead I am going to suggest that you start by taking action on yourself. If you were a top athlete this would make perfect sense to you. You wouldn't dream of trying to run a race without having prepared yourself properly, physically and mentally, so that you were in top form. Yet in our everyday lives we tend to put no emphasis on this type of preparation. We get our papers or ideas together before we do something, but we don't stop to check that we are ready to give our best performance. If you want to be excellent in what you do, this is a vital addition to your repertoire of preparation.

## a state of excellence

We spend most of our lives buffeted by external circumstances that seem to throw us into different moods and states. There are those who are able to move beyond this uncontrolled reaction to external circumstances. They take control of their own state and manage themselves so as to maintain the mood they want. These people have learned how to create a state of excellence.

The difference it makes to the way they lead their lives is tremendous. We all know that when we feel good and when we feel in control we perform better: tasks are easier, problems are solvable, people are more straightforward to deal with and we are prepared for the unexpected. It seems so obvious that I wonder why it isn't the first thing we are taught to do – controlling our own state. In fact, the reverse is true. Most of us are taught that we don't have the right to control our own state!

# looking after yourself

Being in control of your own state begins with looking after yourself, so that you do not over-stretch and put yourself under strain. It is a natural instinct to look after yourself in this way. As small children we do it automatically, but we quickly learn that it is not acceptable.

> Do you remember, as a small child, how you knew when you were hungry, or tired, or needed to go for a walk in the fresh air? And parents, with good intention, said things like:
>
> 'You can't be hungry, it's not 5 o'clock yet.'
> 'Don't go to sleep now – you won't sleep tonight if you do.'
> 'We can't go to the park – it's raining.'

None of these statements made sense to you, because they didn't match your instincts, but you learned to accept that the world doesn't work according to instinct. We quickly learn that we cause less disruption to ourselves and others if we fit in with the external rules rather than follow the messages our bodies give us.

I am not suggesting that you curl up and go to sleep every couple of hours at work – although maybe the workplace would be run more effectively if this were normal practice! Certainly the Japanese are already experimenting with special 'executive nap' areas where senior managers can go and doze for 20 minutes.

What I am suggesting is that you learn again to take more notice of the messages your body gives you, so that you work more effectively with it.

It is, after all, the vehicle that allows you to do what you do. It makes sense to listen to its wisdom rather than put it under strain.

## the effect of ignoring your body's messages

All of us suffer to some degree from ignoring our inner wisdom. The strain caused by not working with our bodies shows as weariness, bad temper, colds and flu, stomach upsets, tension in our muscles, back strain – do I need to go on? When we ignore the body's messages, it shouts louder until we have to take notice.

I used to be someone who worked hard, put in long hours, and neglected myself badly. One winter I had worked through colds and flu, keeping myself going with caffeine and aspirins. I was too exhausted to do much in the evenings, but I wasn't sleeping very well. None the less, I got up every morning and dashed off to work.

Then one morning I woke with terrible pains in my back. I could hardly crawl out of bed, and dragged myself to the phone in utter panic, to call the doctor. When he came and examined me, the doctor said that what was wrong with me was just exhaustion. 'It seems that the only way your body could make you stop was by giving you pains you couldn't ignore. Go to bed for three days, and we'll see what happens.' When I gave in and just stayed in bed, the pains disappeared. And I learned an important lesson.

## how to listen to your own messages

It is worth beginning to take more notice of the messages your body gives you – you could save yourself from reaching the stage where the messages are as blatant and potentially damaging as mine were.

1. *Notice if you feel hungry.* Have some fruit or a biscuit accessible at work, for moments of real hunger.
2. *Notice if you feel tired.* Give yourself a five-minute break and relax by breathing deeply. (If you can't easily do this where you are, visit the loo!)
3. *Notice if your shoulders, face or legs are tense.* Take a deep breath and consciously relax the part(s) of your body where there is tension.

4. *Notice if you need some movement.* Get up and walk somewhere. Use any excuse to do so.
5. *Notice if you need some fresh air.* Go outside for a moment, or at least open a window.
6. *Notice if your face has become 'set'.* Find a reason to laugh – have a funny cartoon nearby to turn to when you need it.

These are neither difficult to do nor time-consuming. They are small remedial actions that will help to retrain you to look after yourself and heed your own body's messages.

> *Decide to listen to your own messages. Begin by setting certain times during the day to stop and assess your state. It may be once an hour, or four times a day. Make a note to yourself in your diary or daily list of tasks which says, 'What do I feel?' Put the six-item checklist on a small card or Post-it Note, until you establish the habit of running through them all automatically. If there are other types of message you begin to notice, add them to the list.*

Every top athlete has this awareness of their body's messages, because if they didn't they would put themselves under unnecessary strain and spoil their performance. We can care for ourselves in a similar way.

# making yourself feel good

Listening to your own natural wisdom will help you avoid causing yourself more strain, so that you become healthier and have more energy, physically and mentally. We can take it a stage further and make ourselves feel good.

Again, we can turn to the example of small children to learn how to optimize our state. Children know how to make themselves feel good, if they are allowed to, by those external rules! They will choose to do things that feed their senses with pleasure and put them in a good mood. In adulthood, we call it having treats, and we tend to restrict it to special occasions or as a special reward. It then becomes something occasional, often expensive, and we have significantly more deprivation than treats! This is both unnecessary and unhealthy. It is good for us to make ourselves feel good:

■ We perform whatever we're doing more effectively.
■ We are more pleasant to be around for others.
■ We have more energy.
■ We are better at dealing with problems and obstacles.
■ We enjoy life more.

## so what are treats?

When we are in the company of a child, we are often amazed by how much they find to delight in in the world. They experience things that we have come to take for granted in a fresh way, and they have a very clear and immediate assessment of what they do and don't like. If you explore this further, you will find that they prefer and notice things that appeal to their five senses: sight, hearing, taste, touch and smell.

> Going for a walk with my son in the country would always reawaken my own awareness. He would notice every tiny wild flower, delighting in the colour and shape and feel of the petals and scent. He heard every bird call and looked up to trace its owner. He followed the sound of the cricket until he found it perched on a stem of grass. He picked up pebbles and stroked their smooth surface; he compared the colour and shape of different leaves. He splashed through puddles, swished through long grass, crunched through autumn leaves, and left his imprint on fresh snow.
>
> As he explored the delights around him, I too would be reminded of the wonders of the everyday world, and would return from the walk feeling energized and revitalized.

These things are the treats that make us feel good: things that make us smile for a moment, which we receive through our five senses. They give us energy and vitality and set us up to be at our best.

As adults, we often forget this, except when we are already feeling good. Only then do we allow ourselves to enjoy what there is around us. When we're feeling bad, however, we tend to deprive ourselves even more, not caring what we wear, or eat, not noticing things we enjoy seeing or hearing.

## treating yourself well

If you want to improve your state and choose to be more resourceful, then you need to start by re-learning how to treat yourself well.

*Identify now six things that can give you pleasure on an everyday basis for each of your senses. Make sure that you choose things you can experience easily, not things you only experience in your annual holiday, or when you have lots of time and money. Here are some examples:*

- *Seeing:* the photo on your bedside table; the flowers in your garden; your pet's beautiful coat; your brightly coloured bedspread; the colours in your living-room; your books on their shelves.
- *Hearing:* the birds singing; a favourite CD; the sound of your partner's voice; the hum of a distant lawnmower; wind in the trees; some wind chimes.
- *Tasting:* fresh coffee; a pineapple; good red wine; tomato soup; fruit cake; buttered toast.
- *Smelling:* your favourite perfume; freshly mown grass; rosemary; freesias; bacon cooking.
- *Feeling/touching:* the feel of a silk shirt; the pebbles on your shelf from the seaside; the cat's fur; the wind on your face; leaves under your feet; the comfort of your bed.

By having lots of treats in a day you begin to have some control over your own mood and state. You choose whether you feel bad or good and are not reliant on external factors. If something drains your energy, you know you can simply and easily begin to replace it.

Again, notice that top athletes look after themselves in this way. They want to keep their mood positive, calm and alert, so that they can give of their best. We also need to be able to give of our best, rather than worrying about whether this is going to be the straw that broke the camel's back.

## a small warning

Having discovered how you can make yourself feel good, do not attempt to do it all the time. This may sound strange: isn't it preferable to feel good? Of course it is, but we also need to allow for the fact that our moods do fluctuate, and that is natural. Sometimes I will feel miserable, or tired, or fed up, and if I allow a space for that mood, it has a chance to pass away. A Buddhist teacher described moods as clouds in the sky – they just pass on if you leave them be. If we try to fight a bad mood, it often persists for even longer, or reappears in some other form. It is not healthy to ignore our moods and pretend that we are always on top form.

However, you can put a time limit on a mood, now you know that you can treat yourself well and lift yourself out of it. The choice of being able to feel good means that you don't have to get stuck in a mood which isn't useful to you.

# creating the state you want

Besides knowing how to make yourself feel good, you can also learn how to consciously give yourself the right attitude to perform well in a particular situation. This is something that people do unconsciously some of the time, and when you understand how it works, you can use it to prepare yourself whenever you want to. I call it using triggers, because it involves having a particular stimulus that automatically produces a particular reaction in your body and your mind to create the state you want.

## what are triggers?

Triggers are external or internal influences that automatically produce a particular mood in you. They are directly linked to our senses, like treats. So treats are all triggers that make us feel good.

There are other triggers that may create slightly different states in us. Here are some examples:

- The sound of a stream gurgling over rocks and pebbles – makes me calm and peaceful.
- The sight of a traffic jam – winds me up.
- The taste of conference pears – makes me alert.
- The smell of a train station – makes me anxious.
- The feel of wet grass under my bare feet – makes me energetic.

You will notice that these are not necessarily logical. All triggers have their effect because they are linked to memories of specific experiences. They happen to represent that experience for us, and remind our bodies and minds of what we were like at that particular moment. We automatically resume that state. Particular triggers will have different effects on different people, depending on their previous experience.

> I wanted to say thank you to my staff for working with me on a particular project, and brought a box of chocolates to the meeting. One said he didn't like chocolates – they reminded him of being ill in hospital. Another looked at me suspiciously – she thought I was bribing them into doing yet more work. A third took a chocolate, looked at it, bit into it and savoured the taste – he made us laugh with his sensual delight, and he said that chocolates made him feel very pampered and looked after. The fourth person said that presents of any kind made him feel valued, and the fifth said just the sight of chocolates made her feel fat and frumpy and fed up!

# how do you use triggers?

Most people don't consciously use triggers – they just happen. We may not even realize that something that is associated with a particular mood from our past has just set off that mood again in us. We all know, for example, that certain pieces of music make us nostalgic, or energized, or calm, but we don't usually use that music to deliberately create that mood in ourselves.

Once you do decide to create the mood you want, you increase the control you have over yourself a hundredfold, because you can use the good triggers and offset those that don't create the right mood for you.

*Begin by identifying some triggers that work for you in ways you find useful:*

- *What reminds you to feel resourceful, able to cope with anything?*
- *What makes you feel energetic?*
- *What reminds you of being calm?*
- *What reminds you of being on top form?*
- *What brings you to a state of alertness?*
- *What represents confidence for you?*

You may have more than one trigger, or ones that reach different senses. For example, bouncing a ball makes me feel energetic: the sight of it, the sensation of it and the sound of it.

You may also want to add in some other states or attitudes you would like to create in yourself automatically, such as focused, a state for writing, a state for presenting and so on.

What do you do if you don't already have a trigger? You think back to a time you had the attitude you want to be able to re-create. As you remember the experience, notice what there was in that experience that would serve as a trigger. What catches your attention, via one of your senses? Use that as the trigger.

Athletes often have some form of talisman that they carry around with them, or a ritual about how they get dressed for action – different ways of setting a trigger to help create the mood they want.

Once you have identified some triggers, you can consciously practise using them. Some will be items you can easily have with you – a photograph, a particular pen, for example. Others require you to use your imagination – I cannot carry a babbling stream around with me but I can imagine the sound of it in my head, and this is just as effective. When I want to feel calm, I spend a moment or two imagining the sound of that stream, and I automatically calm down.

It takes only a breath-space to use a trigger to change your state, and it gives you control of how you act and react in any situation.

# the use of thoughts

How we talk to ourselves constitutes a powerful form of trigger. We all conduct some form of internal commentary, and it can be consciously used to adjust our state. Be aware of what you are telling yourself about a situation, and consciously make your thoughts constructive.

A colleague was clearly getting more and more anxious about giving a presentation to the team. I asked him what his thoughts were about it. He said, 'To be honest, I keep thinking that they will be very critical of what I have to say. I'm not sure I can express what I want to say clearly and I'm feeling panicky.'

I suggested to him that he realigned his thoughts to be more useful to him, and suggested some possibilities: 'I have given good presentations before. I know what I want to say. My colleagues are sympathetic because they know what it feels like to have to give a presentation. I care about my subject matter, and people will respect the genuineness of the message.'

He started to laugh, and began to add some other thoughts along similar lines. He was now talking himself into giving a good presentation.

*Take something you feel anxious or unsure about, and begin to talk to yourself (in your head) about it in a more constructive way. Use phrases like: 'I have succeeded before', 'I can . . .', 'I want to . . .'. If a negative thought occurs, think of a counter to it, for example: 'I'm not very good at concentrating, but I can concentrate when I'm playing golf, so why not here?'*

So often we allow ourselves to fall into a negative spiral of thoughts. Since thoughts do have so much effect on us, we might as well use their power constructively!

# how will this make me an effective 21st century manager?

Did this chapter seem at a bit of a tangent? 'I've convinced myself that I want to develop, let's get on with it!' is how many task-driven managers react. In reality, learning to resource yourself is fundamental to your development. It is the starting point for all the other aspects of development you will undertake.

By learning to manage yourself more effectively through methods such as these, you are already beginning to develop some of the characteristics of the effective manager:

- You are becoming more self-aware.
- You are providing a model for self-management.
- You are learning to think positively.
- You are allowing yourself to be enthusiastic and real, in a constructive way.

## conclusion

When people talk about preparation, they usually mean doing things. Here we are talking about how you are rather than what you are going to do.

By learning to take more care of yourself, to take some control over your state, you are enhancing the way you are, your being.

It is a form of preparation that would seem obvious to a top athlete, but is rarely considered by managers. Yet we know that we too give our peak performances when we are physically and mentally at our best.

Begin today to listen to your own body, to allow yourself the treats to make you feel good, and to consciously use triggers to create the state you want. You have begun the process of becoming an effective 21st century manager.

The ideas in this chapter may also remind you to take some time out – working all the time isn't healthy and doesn't lead to top performance. If there is no balance between your work life and your home life, then you are out of balance. No one wants their epitaph to be: 'This person spent their life at the office.'

# relating **to yourself**

Before we can relate effectively to others, we need to learn how to be comfortable with ourselves. There's no one more difficult to deal with than the person who has not established his or her own integrity.

The word 'integrity' means wholeness, and it applies to people who act with consistency to their own values and beliefs. They do not just fit in with others, or contradict themselves. You know where you stand with them.

In order to have your own integrity, you need to sort out what you stand for and be comfortable with it.

## what do I stand for?

Most of us don't actually think about this. It only comes to the fore when we are put into a situation where we find ourselves unable to accept what's being presented to us, where our core values are being fundamentally disregarded. We generally live with some degree of compromise, and cope with the discomfort which that produces.

> I remember being quite shocked when a manager I knew, who had been made redundant, said to me, 'It's a relief, Di, to be finally free of that company.' I had expected him to be upset and resentful. His explanation? 'I'm a nice person really. I like to treat people well, and I believe that most people work well if you treat them with respect. But in that company you had to be a "hard man" if you were a manager, and it didn't suit me. I feel I can be human again, and maybe somewhere there's a job I can do where I can be more myself.'

I now know that his reaction is not that unusual. We may learn to live with the discomfort of not having our integrity, but it causes us long-term damage, and certainly doesn't bring out the best in us. By becoming conscious of what we stand for and refusing to accept the discomfort, we do both ourselves and others a favour.

## your core values

To clarify for yourself what you stand for, you begin by sorting out what really matters to you. It is important to take time over this and to be honest with yourself. No one else will see what you come up with, so you can leave out all the things you think you *should* care about. The question is:

*'If there were no other influences affecting me, how would I want to be in the world?'*

To answer this, you can consider a series of categories:

- my lifestyle;
- my environment;
- the way I'm treated by others;
- the way I behave towards others;
- the importance of material things;
- the importance of spiritual things;
- the importance of relationships;
- the importance of feelings;
- the importance of social issues.

*Take the categories listed and make a note of what really matters to you in those categories, if anything. Use these questions to help you:*

- *How would you like to live your daily routine? What do you want as regular components in your life?*
- *What sort of environment do you prefer to be in?*
- *How would you like others to be with you?*
- *How do you want to be in relation to others?*
- *To what degree do material comforts matter to you?*
- *Are there spiritual values that matter to you?*
- *How do you want to feel in your everyday life? To what extent do you want to take feelings into account?*
- *What social issues are important to you?*

Make your own list, adding in anything else that matters to you which you feel is not really covered by the categories I've offered. Now consider your notes and ask yourself how you would rank them in order of importance. I know this is difficult, but you need to establish for yourself which are the vital few. Identify your top five or top ten.

You may find that this exercise raises all sorts of questions for you, like:

- 'X is very important to me, but I only really live it at weekends.'
- 'I don't really expect most people to treat me with respect, although I'd prefer it.'
- 'I'm not sure what's really important to me.'

When you first stop and consider your core values, you may find that there are more questions than answers, but it does begin the process of sorting them out and starting to take notice of how much you live by them.

## living our core values

Deciding to live your core values as much as possible allows you to be more comfortable with yourself. It also enhances the respect you gain from others. As Shakespeare said:

> This above all: to thine own self be true,
> And it must follow, as the night the day,
> Thou canst not then be false to any man.

We call it things like being genuine, being straight, when we encounter people who are living their core values. It is much easier to deal with someone who has that integrity.

### how do I know if I'm living by my core values?
Having become conscious of what matters to us, we automatically become more aware of times when what we're doing doesn't fit. You begin to notice discomfort that you previously put up with. One area where it is most noticeable is in the way people treat you.

If you want to be treated with respect and liked, but notice that this is not the case, you can use this as an indicator that you have some work to do on the way you treat others. This may sound strange, but we usually receive similar treatment to that which we give out – people respond in kind. So if I want to be treated with respect, I must treat others with respect, and they will begin to respond in the same way.

### organizational constraints
Many people, like the manager I spoke of earlier, feel that they have to put on a front of being a 'hard man', because that is what is expected of them in the organization. There is no doubt that there are still companies that

demand short-term results and see 'hard' management as the way to achieve them. However, it is gradually becoming clear that being tough may give short-term results, but doesn't give the results required for longer-term survival into the 21st century.

There is a myth that if you're pleasant with people and show concern, you lose respect and they don't bother to work hard for you. I would suggest that you examine your own experience to counteract this myth.

> I was changing jobs and would have a new boss. My old boss said: 'Oh, he's a soft touch. He won't push you as hard as I did.' It was true. The new boss didn't push me as hard. He was friendly, approachable, and always had time to chat to me about what was going on, inside and out of work. And I found that I worked hard to be the best at the job, because he gave credit for you doing so.

*Who have you worked well for? Was it the 'hard man' or was it the person who had integrity and treated you well? And how do you compare with these stereotypes? How are you reducing the pressure of organizational constraints for your team?*

Most of our core values *can* be lived to within organizations, even if it isn't the norm. Occasionally you may come across unethical practice that is accepted within the company. We all have to make choices about what we do in this circumstance. I would suggest that most of such practice comes from a belief that it leads to some short-term gain, and if you can come up with an alternative, more ethical approach that delivers results, it will be accepted.

Both staff and customers prefer and respond positively to ethical behaviour. That represents a large proportion of the population, from which one could infer that we all prefer to behave ethically if we have the choice. It is in both your personal and organization's long-term interest to live your core values.

## what is your purpose?

The other part of establishing what you stand for is to be clear about your purpose. There are many terms that suggest this: vision, mission, intention, motivation – all have some elements of this in their meaning.

I think it is simply clarifying what you are being a manager for. Most of us become managers almost by default. It's the next step on the ladder, or it's the obvious job to take. We tend not to stop and think about what makes us purposeful in the role. Yet our purpose defines the way in which we approach the role, and has a significant effect on our performance. If you consider this in a different context, you will see what I mean.

> If my purpose in gardening is to get it done quickly so that I don't get nagged, then I will do as little as possible, have a low-maintenance garden, and not bother to learn about or enjoy plants.
>
> If my purpose is for my garden to look better than the neighbours', I will buy showy plants and take a great deal of care of the areas that can be seen by others, but neglect other parts of the garden.
>
> If my purpose is to create a garden I can enjoy, I will turn it into a labour of love, and experiment with different plants and arrangements.

## defining your purpose

A way of clarifying your purpose for yourself is to consider what you would like others to say about you as their manager. For example:

'Sue was a manager who provided the support and guidance that allowed me to do my best.'
Your purpose would then be:
'To enable my team to do their best, by providing appropriate support and guidance.'

*Write down a few lines defining your purpose in being a manager. Use the format: 'My purpose is to . . ., by . . .'*

We have spent quite a long time examining what you stand for. It is vital in being comfortable with yourself to be clear about what matters to you and gives you purpose in what you're doing. Often people think that flexibility means that you must be prepared to compromise your values, but if you use the metaphor of a tree swaying in the wind, you will notice that its roots and trunk are firm, and it is the branches that move. Similarly with humans, we need a strong core of values and purpose that allows us to be flexible in our behaviours, yet consistent with our principles.

# giving yourself permission

When we decide to live our values and be true to ourselves, we discover that we feel more comfortable with ourselves in some ways and less comfortable in others. We feel better for having more integrity, but we often bump up against other norms in the organization which seem to push us to compromise. It is important to be kind to yourself when this happens.

## forgiving yourself

You need to accept that sometimes you will go with the compromise. We are only human and we can't always be perfect! It is not helpful to berate yourself when you fail to live up to your own expectations. This type of reaction so often leads to giving up altogether, or lowering your standards.

> Learn from children. When they are learning to walk, they may take a tumble. They don't then give up on walking and decide to settle for crawling, nor do they berate themselves for falling. They have a little rest, dust themselves down, and have another go.

When we realize we have 'fallen', we need to take the same attitude. After all, the realization itself is progress – before I clarified my purpose, I didn't even know if I was failing to fulfil it! In fact, I have a teacher who recommends that you reward yourself for noticing that you have not met your own expectations, rather than beat yourself up!

## taking it a step at a time

There may be some situations where it is easier for you to stand up for your core values than others. Practise living your values and purpose in these ones first. By developing the habit where it is easy, you will find that it gradually becomes automatic, and you will begin to apply it in more difficult situations.

> When we're learning to drive, we don't start off in the middle of a busy town. It is much easier to learn the basics where there isn't much traffic to contend with. Once the basic skills of driving become automatic, we can begin to apply them when there are more things to be aware of.

*How can you start to fully live your values and purpose at work? In which contexts will it be easiest? It may be with your immediate team, or with your peers.*

# getting support

We all need feedback to tell us that we are doing the right thing. It is not enough to feel in ourselves that we are on the right track. We want others to encourage us as well.

Often this form of support is not given automatically. There are two ways you can get this support for yourself.

## asking for feedback

Make a point of asking your staff and your peers to notice whenever you are living your values, to encourage you to do so. Don't just ask for feedback in general. People have a tendency to give you negatives rather than positives, and that can make you feel worse!

## identifying allies

Most of us find it easier to develop ourselves when there are others who are committed to the same thing. Look around you and find out who else is working at living their core values. It may be other managers, or some of your staff, or even people outside your workplace.

When I was a young and inexperienced teacher, I felt that it was important to develop the children I taught in whatever way I could. Within the staffroom I met only cynicism. 'You'll soon get over that!' was the general attitude. But one other teacher felt as I did, and we would spend lunch-times together, sharing ideas and beliefs. I also started working in a youth club, where the leader was as committed as I was to the development of the potential of young people. He encouraged me to attend a seminar where I met more people who shared my views. By using this network for support, I felt more able to maintain my principles regarding my students.

*What allies do you have in living your core values? Look around and identify a support network for yourself, both in and out of work.*

If you find that there are not many, then actively look for opportunities to extend your network of support. And don't forget that your allies may not be people in a direct sense. I have tapes and books that are important allies for me. They encourage me to keep going when I'm feeling isolated, and remind me that there are others doing what I'm doing, even if I don't know them personally.

# enjoying your individuality

We are all different. We have different upbringings, experiences and interpretations of our experiences, which make us unique. One of the delights of human beings is that everyone has something about them that makes them stand out from the crowd.

Sadly, we are prone to hide our individuality and conform to the patterns we see around us, because there is a common belief that you get by in life by conforming. And of course there is some truth in this: you do get by, generally! However, if you look at those who are excellent in what they do, you will find that they are all people who express and delight in their own individuality.

It is hard to relate well to yourself if you are trying to act as if you were someone else!

How you express your individuality may vary. It may be through the clothes you wear, or by the way you set up your immediate environment. It may be in the way you talk about things, or the way you react to situations.

> I have a good sense of humour. I enjoy telling stories to the groups I work with. I am informal and relaxed in my approach to things. I'm lively and pretty optimistic. I express my individuality by the clothes I wear, my long dangly earrings, and a tendency to take my shoes off when I'm working.

*What makes you special and unique? Identify your favourite personal characteristics. If you find this hard to do, imagine your best friend describing you and what makes you special. Now identify how you express your individuality – and if you don't, how you could!*

It is important that you find some way to say 'This is me!' which is distinct from others. It allows you to feel that the whole you is present in what you are doing and to be more comfortable with yourself.

## conclusion

Learning to relate well to yourself is the first step to relating more effectively to others around you. We cannot be comfortable with others until we are comfortable with ourselves.

It also brings out in us some more of the qualities that are seen as essential to the 21st century manager. We become more self-aware, we demonstrate that we have ethics and values, and we are more real as human beings.

It is the real you that those who like and respect you relate to, not a partial you, with some characteristics suppressed. When you think back over your own experience, I am sure that you will find that those you most admire, respect and like are all people who are being true to themselves and their individuality.

These qualities are inherent in us, and it is merely a question of allowing them to show and be used as assets in our work, rather than hiding them because we fear non-conformity.

# the **way you think**

All that we have considered so far has some relevance to the way you think. I have encouraged you to consider your beliefs, your values and your ability to use your thoughts constructively. I would now like to take it a stage further and consider in a little more depth the importance of your way of thinking for your effectiveness as a 21st century manager.

## thinking positively

Thinking positively is listed as one of the key characteristics of the 21st century manager. People are often wary of this, as they see it as meaning that you refuse to accept current reality and view the world through rose-tinted spectacles.

If we take it literally, thinking positively means that you notice what's possible, rather than what's not possible. This is not the same as being unrealistic. It is simply a different way of filtering the information.

> I remember being in a yoga class years ago. 'I can't do this position,' I said to the teacher. He smiled and said, 'What can you do?' I showed him how far I could get with the position, and he said, 'So all we need to do is find a way to relax your back muscles so that your legs can move a little more – try this.' And he adjusted my position slightly. I found that I could take up the position after all. My negative thinking led me to giving up. His positive thinking led to action that made it possible.

Have you ever had this kind of help to shift you from negative thinking to recognizing possibilities – or, of course, done it for yourself? Notice how negative thinking leads to inaction, and positive thinking leads to action.

*Think of something you believe you can't do or achieve. What can you do that is part way to achieving it? What else can you do that would make it possible for you to achieve it?*

## asking the right questions

To train ourselves into thinking constructively, we need to learn to ask the right questions. Many of our thoughts are a response to an unvoiced question. If we become aware of the questions we can alter them and thus our response or thought.

> If your thought is: 'I knew this project wouldn't work out because I didn't have enough time to do it,' then the unvoiced question is: 'Why didn't it work?'
>
> If the question had been: 'How can I make it work?', the thought might be: 'I need to clear some more time if I want to make this project work.' That would then lead to another question: 'How can I do that?'

Notice how different the thought is in response to the different unvoiced question. We tend to spend a lot of time asking ourselves, 'Why did things go wrong?' This is not a useful focus. The question should be: 'How can I make things work?' The first question analyses the past and focuses on the problem. The second question looks forward and produces solutions to the problem.

## the 'why' question

In my training work, I often suggest to people that they ban 'why' from their vocabulary. This is deliberately provocative and I always have people defending their use of 'why'. Yet after some practise in asking more useful questions, people begin to realize that 'why' may not be as helpful as they thought it was.

Whenever we ask 'why' we are implying that we don't agree or think something is wrong. After all, if someone does something that makes sense to us, we will rarely ask them why they did it, because it's obvious to us. Because of this, the response to being asked 'why' is usually defensive and often attempts to blame something or someone other than the person answering. Even if our intention was merely to get more information, people will still tend to react defensively, finding justifications for what happened.

There is a different reaction to 'How did that happen?' or 'What happened to produce this result?' These are more neutral questions that produce information about the process.

---

A manager in a manufacturing company had learned to use the Japanese quality check, which includes the 'five whys', to get to the root cause of the problem. A serious defect was allowed to continue down the assembly line, with everyone working around it. When it eventually came to light, at the final audit stage, he started asking why it had been allowed through. Typical answers were:

- I didn't notice it.
- The line was going too fast and I'd have been in trouble if I hadn't done my job.
- It's not my job to report defects in that part.
- You said we had to get the numbers up this week.
- I thought someone else must have said it was OK.
- I didn't want to get John into trouble.

What he didn't get was the real reason for the defect going through. Eventually he took a deep breath, calmed down, went to the team leader and asked, 'What exactly happened here?' The team leader explained that the team member who would usually pick up on that defect was absent, and the person filling in didn't realize how serious it was.

The manager then asked: 'How can we prevent it from happening again?' The team leader responded that she wanted to train the whole team in each other's jobs, so that they would be more able to fill in for each other effectively and would notice if something was wrong, but he had told her that there wasn't time. She also wanted to establish team responsibility for the product, but the reward system still worked on an individual basis, so that was difficult.

He now had more useful information, and the choice of acting on it to solve the problem, or of course continuing to look for someone to blame!

---

Whether we are asking ourselves or others the questions, we need to ensure that the questions help us to think constructively.

# systemic thinking

In the last example I gave, the manager shifted from 'blame' thinking to systemic thinking. Quality improvement gurus have been saying for a long time that most problems stem from the system rather than the people. Duran suggested that 85 per cent of problems were system related; Deming increased that to 94 per cent. Yet most organizations still look for someone to blame if something goes wrong.

As managers we need to begin to shift our way of approaching things so that we reduce the blame culture and recognize that it is frequently the process that causes the problems – people's behaviour is merely the symptom. This is more challenging in one sense. It is easier to find someone to blame and to tell them to change their behaviour. However, as a solution this will only work short term. The problem will reappear in some other form, and we end up with the constant fire-fighting that is a feature of so many managers' jobs.

By tracing the problem back to its source, we can make changes that allow people to perform better and which are genuinely empowering.

A manager was struggling with the issue of keeping her papers organized. She always seemed to have piles of stuff to be filed away, and often couldn't find what she was looking for. At first she blamed her PA for not keeping the filing up to date. The PA took the blame and conscientiously did the filing. The manager still couldn't find things, and what's more, her post now arrived on her desk later in the morning.

When we looked at what was happening, we discovered that the process was very convoluted. Her PA opened her post and gave it to her. She then sorted through it for anything urgent and dealt with that, leaving the rest on one side. During the day, she added any reports, meeting notes, etc that she received to the pile. At lunch-time she went through the piles, pulled out items that her PA could action, attached a note and handed them over. Towards the end of the day, the PA would report on her actions, bring in letters to sign, etc. Then the manager would go through the remaining pile, sort them for filing or throwing away, and hand the filing to the PA. If she didn't have time, the papers would wait till the next day and be added to the pile.

No wonder there were problems! When we brought the PA in and discussed how we would improve the process, we were able to devise a much more effective system for dealing with the paperwork.

*Take a problem you currently face, as a manager. Work through what exactly happens that leads to the problem. Identify ways you could improve the process to improve the result. (If you want more information on methods for doing this, see Peter Senge in the recommended reading list, p. 208.)*

## forward system thinking

This way of thinking about things doesn't only give you a more useful approach to problems you already have, it also helps you to avoid problems in the future. When you decide to take an action, stop and think it through first. What will the consequences of that action be – for you, for others, for customers, for the business? Remember that there are immediate consequences – the obvious results – but also longer-term consequences – the subsequent effects.

> Any gardener knows that before you plant something new in the garden you need to consider its long-term effect. Filling a space with fast-growing firs may look good in the short term, but they will soon leach the ground around them and create a large space where nothing else can grow easily. Bulbs planted in the autumn only show their result in the spring. In gardening, you have to think about the long-term results.

So often decisions are made in business to give a short-term result, and the other consequences are not taken into account. A training budget is cut to save costs, and staff are not given the help they need to continue to perform effectively. A new piece of machinery is purchased, and the knock-on effect of marrying this new technology to what already exists is not properly considered. No doubt you have numerous examples of your own!

*Reconsider a decision you are about to make. Have you thought through the consequences for next week, next month, next year? Have you considered the effect on you, on your staff, on your customers?*

By developing our ability to think systemically, we not only improve our practice, we also begin to educate others in this way of thinking because we use different justifications for our actions and decisions. We talk in terms of process improvement and longer-term effects, instead of bouncing from problems to short-term solutions and back again to resulting problems.

Further, we become better at noticing the real leverage points for making a positive difference, instead of dealing just with the symptoms of something not working properly. We see the inter-relationships and patterns that underlie the presenting behaviour, rather than just the immediate sign of a problem. As Senge says: 'Ultimately [systems thinking] simplifies life by helping us see the deeper patterns lying behind the event and the details.'

# remembering the customer

Closely linked to systemic thinking is our need to be constantly aware of the customer or end-user when we are planning. There are many examples of the result of lack of customer awareness:

- housing estates with no shopping or leisure facilities;
- computer manuals;
- offices with no natural light.

Technical improvements do not necessarily improve the lot of the customer and it is ultimately the customer who maintains the business, not the technicians. The concept of customer focus has been around for a while now, but it is still not given the priority it needs. Often those who are trained in customer satisfaction are those who have least control over the product or service – they may be front-line in selling it to the customer, but they do not design, produce or deliver it.

Systemic thinking encourages us to consider the effect on the customer of a decision we make or an action we take. It prompts us to be aware of the wider consequences.

## who are the customers?

It is important to remember that you always have more than one customer. I would suggest that the first customer you consider is yourself. You are the first person affected by a decision and that in itself will affect the way you deal with others.

Then there are end-users: the people who finally end up with your product or service. There is a simple question to ask yourself here: 'If I were my customer, what would I want and expect?'

I've always been fascinated by the fact that people will replicate behaviours that they have personally found unacceptable – how can they ignore their own customer feedback? Managers give the same boring presentations their managers gave to them; after complaining about others' rudeness on the phone, they are rude to their own staff; they complain about the impossibility of getting hold of their accountant, and then refuse to speak to colleagues who are trying to contact them. It is as if we live our lives in separate compartments, and have no common sense to link them together.

These examples are fairly obvious, but there are others that are less direct. My favourite example is manuals for technical equipment. These will usually be written by people who understand the technology. They describe what to do in terms and in an order that makes sense to them, but to the layperson, the language and descriptions are far too complex.

There is a third group of customers: they are all those who are part of the process of getting the product or service from you to the end-user. This may be staff, colleagues, other departments, other businesses. You may write a manual that does speak the layperson's language, but if you don't present it in a way that makes it easy for the printer to print it accurately, your customer still won't be satisfied.

---

The manager of a hairdressing salon was hearing comments from customers that they would like him to stay open later in the evening so they could come after work.

He first conducted a more general survey to find out what proportion of his customers shared this view. He then considered the effect on himself if he were to work longer hours. He was already over-stretched, so he decided to operate a shift system – the same number of hours per staff member, but at different times, to cover two late-night openings per week. He now had to consider how to suggest this to his staff in a way that would appeal to them. He decided that staffing a late night would be packaged with a half-day on Saturdays, as he knew that some staff, himself included, would like this deal and see it as an improvement. By this careful planning he satisfied *all* his customers.

---

You will notice in this example that the first action was to ask the customer. This is the quickest way to find out what will make a difference and what is really required, and can be used for every level of customer.

# visionary thinking

I have discussed before the importance of being able to envision ideals. Many managers get caught up in their everyday work, simply trying to keep things running smoothly. The pressure of this maintenance can push aside the need for larger aims.

Yet one of the central characteristics of leaders is that they are visionary. The word implies that they have an ideal they are aiming for, and that they communicate that vision. This is more than incremental improvement – it is the big leaps forward in practice, process and possibilities. It requires imagination and inspiration rather than just logic.

Most managers I've met have a vision, although they tend not to use the word. They may express it as a wish-list, or fantasy, rather than as the driver for their work. Visions consist of two parts:

- What we will achieve.
- How we will achieve it.

Here's an example:

> This department will receive only praise from our customers. We will offer excellent quality, and will go beyond customer expectations. We will be innovative and creative in our approach. We will work co-operatively together and always be developing new ways of working. People will want to come to work, and others will queue up to join the department.

Sometimes, of course, the visions are broader, depending on the position you have in the company. Their purpose is to extend the boundaries of your thinking about what's possible and to give you something to aim for.

> *How would you express your vision for your area of responsibility? Note it down, being careful in how you express it. Remember the section on positive thinking earlier in this chapter, and express your vision of what you would like to be achieved and how you would like your team to be, not what you don't want.*

Visions are ideals, and it is important that they go beyond the immediately possible. As the saying goes: 'Shoot for the stars and you may reach the moon; shoot only for the horizon, and you may hit the ground.' They help us to stretch and grow or to develop a dynamic, so that our work is constantly developing and we are always looking for ways of stepping closer to the ideal.

The vision allows you to move outside the tramlines of everyday action and have a different perspective on how you might move from current reality towards the ideal.

Excellent leaders think 'outside the box' yet still bear in mind what they have to deal with currently. (You will find more on developing and using your vision in Chapter 12.)

# creative thinking

You will notice that the implication in the above section is that the practical visionary can think creatively as well as rationally. Thinking creatively requires a different approach to using your brain. We are not normally encouraged to think creatively, because we have been taught to look for 'right answers' in a logical fashion.

To shift our brain into this gear, we need to become more playful in our thoughts. Again, this comes naturally to children. Give a child a spoon and ask them what they could use it for, and they will come up with lots of ideas: digging, pretending it's a rocket, making a bridge for cars, a missile thrower – the list goes on and on. As adults we tend to narrow our focus, and say it's for stirring or for eating. Great inventions came from people using their imaginations, looking at things in a different way and experimenting with alternatives.

> My hairdresser was looking for ways to attract new customers. He had an upstairs to the shop that wasn't being used for anything except storage. He decided to set it up as a space for children, with murals, toys and videos, so parents could have their hair done and have their children happily occupied and out of the way. That's creative thinking!

*Take a problem you have at present. It may be one of those that nags away at you but isn't serious enough to need immediate action. Play with ways of making a difference to it by asking yourself, 'How many ways could I make a difference to this issue?' and finding at least five. Look at it as if you were a child, accepting 'silly' ideas that come to you as well as the obvious logical ones. And if you're brave enough, try out a 'silly' idea!*

If you can develop the habit of asking yourself how many ways you can think of doing something, you will automatically increase your creativity. You can also deliberately choose to use different perspectives. I have already suggested that you consider things from the point of view of the customer. You can add to this other categories: a child, a sage, someone who knows nothing of history and habits, a Martian – no doubt you can think of some of your own.

# forward thinking

You will notice that most of the forms of thinking I have covered so far are forward thinking. That is, they use thinking to make a difference for the future. It is far more useful to expend your energy on planning to make a difference than to think about what has happened and to wish it had been different.

This doesn't mean that you don't review what has happened – it means that you use the review as your starting point for the main thrust of your thinking. Analysis of the past is only useful if it leads to making a difference in the future.

I always suggest to people a simple formula for encouraging their brain to automatically shift from analysis to action – you might like to try it out for yourself.

*Review your day briefly in your mind. Think of one thing you did well, and imagine the next time you will do the same thing or use the same process again.*

*Now remember something that didn't go so well. Review it briefly, then ask yourself, 'What would I do differently next time to improve that situation?' When you have an idea, imagine yourself carrying it out the next time you hit a similar situation.*

# conclusion

There are whole books about ways of improving our use of our ability to think (see the reading list on p. 207 for some recommendations) and I have just skimmed the surface in this chapter.

Taking control of the way we think about things and learning to use the various ways of thinking are vital prerequisites for excellent leadership. In our list of qualities we have: a visionary; awareness of current reality; systemic thinking and thinking positively. This amounts to a third of the essential qualities. By taking the small steps in practice that I have suggested, you will begin to enhance your use of thought as a means of enhancing your leadership skills.

# being **a learner**

Do you work for a 'learning organization'? More and more businesses are claiming this title for themselves as we move towards the 21st century. There is no doubt that organizations do need to become learning organizations – the rate of change is now so fast that anyone who isn't learning is being left behind. However, this is not merely a titular change: it requires a revolution in traditional working practice. And you are the leaders of the revolution!

A true learning organization has learning as a way of life, for everyone involved in it. They are learning from everyday experiences, learning from mistakes, continually developing their processes and systems and looking for new possibilities all the time. This can hardly be said of most organizational cultures at the moment. There is still a strong blame culture that discourages people from experimenting or risking trying something new. As effective managers in the 21st century, you are going to have to set the example of being an enthusiastic and constant learner again.

## the image of the learner

Picture a learner to yourself. What do you see? A learner driver maybe, slow and clumsy in their management of the car. Or someone giving a presentation for the first time, embarrassed and hesitant.

We have a strongly developed view of learners as those who are stumbling until they finally get it right and can take their place fully fledged and no longer embarrassed by their lack of skill.

This image of a learner is one that few of us wish to emulate! It is seen as an uncomfortable position to be in, and we prefer to keep such states to ourselves. To be open to being a learner may make you feel very vulnerable and exposed.

## revising the image

So the first action we need to take, if we are to be learners in a conscious sense is to revise the image we have of learners. This requires us to consciously search for some different pictures of being a learner, using our own experience to help us to evidence the state of learning in a positive way.

Begin by remembering your own good experiences as a learner. At first some people struggle with this, because the old image of a learner is so powerfully implanted. Often our best examples are not within the formal education setting, where we were being taught, but our informal learning, where we were more relaxed.

> Learning French at school was hard work, but our teacher was enthusiastic and I put in the effort. Then I went on an exchange visit to Paris. When I first arrived, I felt very embarrassed at my lack of skill in spoken French. The family I stayed with were lovely. They encouraged me to have a go, and corrected my mistakes gently and with humour. Within days my spoken French was far more fluent, I was prepared to try to communicate even when I wasn't sure of my ground, and I was continually asking them how to say new things. I was enjoying being a learner.

*What are your examples of good learning experiences? Note down too how you were as a learner: how you felt, what you did, even how you looked.*

As you explore good experiences of learning you begin to develop a new image of a learner, yet it is not alien to us – in fact it is very familiar:

■ enthusiastic;
■ interested;
■ exploring;
■ experimenting;
■ having fun;
■ wanting to learn more.

Now watch a child: this is how we all are as young children – natural learners. You get the feeling that it's what we're designed to do – after all, children don't say, 'Oh, walking/talking is too hard – I give up!' They enjoy the process of gradually absorbing the method by example and encouragement, and experiment with it until they develop their own individual style. Their curiosity leads them to a delight in learning new things and exploring different possibilities, until the cultural norm of learning takes hold of them.

Being a childlike learner, remembering our own good experiences of learning, allows us to develop a revised image of the learner.

# developing our learning skills

When we went to school, teaching was something that was done to us, which was effective to very differing degrees. What few people learn at school is how to learn – the focus is on being taught. As adults we can consciously develop our learning skills by recognizing what works for us, and taking some control over the process instead of being passive recipients.

## how we learn best

It is important to use our experience of effective learning to identify what makes it easy and enjoyable for us to be a learner.

*What was it about your good learning experiences that made the difference? Think through some of your own examples and identify some factors that they share. For instance:*

- *It was relevant to me at the time.*
- *I was given encouragement.*
- *There was plenty of opportunity to practise.*
- *The instructions were very clear.*
- *I could go at my own pace.*
- *There was an atmosphere of fun.*

By identifying the factors that make a difference to us as learners, we can begin to take control of the learning process. It gives us some criteria for selecting formal learning events, and ideas of what we need to create for ourselves in informal learning opportunities.

## what we learn from

We all vary in the way we switch on to learning. For one person, it is the formal event that wakes up the learner in them. For another, it is books or audiotapes. Another will learn most from informal conversations with others.

It is worth considering your main source(s) of learning, because it makes sense to concentrate on those that will appeal to the learner in you the most. Notice that I use the word 'appeal'. To be a learner, you need to follow emotion, not logic, in your choice of methods. You want learning to be easy, natural and enjoyable again, as it was when you were a small child. I always feel a little worried when people tell me that they're taking a course or reading a certain book because they feel they should. We should not feel obliged to learn – it is usually the least successful form of learning for us. They may be better off doing something that may have less external recognition, but may enhance their learning significantly.

Here are some of the sources of learning you may enjoy:

- lectures/talks;
- workshops;
- informal task groups;
- books;
- audiotapes;
- videotapes;
- interactive computer programs;
- biographies/histories;
- visits to different people/places;
- trying things out on your own with instruction manuals;
- conferences;
- keeping a weekly learning log;
- observing others who do it well.

You may be able to think of others.

*Identify your two or three favourite ways of learning. When did you last use them?*

## when we learn

The truth is you are always learning, whether you realize it or not. The question is rather, are you in control of and using your learning? We cannot help but absorb information and draw conclusions about it which affect our behaviour. It is the nature of the beast. We may not call it learning, because there is no obvious 'new' subject, but in fact it is the most common form of learning.

Most of the time we do not learn entirely new things; we develop further our knowledge or skills in areas where we have a basic awareness already.

This is developmental learning and it enables us to deepen or enrich what we already have. It is particularly powerful in learning how to behave or react. However, we need to become conscious of this type of learning and choose to direct it and use it well; otherwise, it may result in us stagnating:

- Have you learned that you can sit through some meetings and just doodle, and no one cares?
- Have you learned not to ask questions that might make you look stupid?
- Have you learned to look busy so no one bothers you?
- Have you learned how to approach colleagues if you want them to do something?

*Identify five or six key behaviours you have learned in this way, and then ask yourself if they add value for you. If they don't, ask yourself what it would be more useful to learn.*

The real question is: does your learning enrich your repertoire and serve you well in your own development?

We are constantly surrounded by opportunities to learn. It is up to us to choose to use the opportunities to develop ourselves.

# being a dynamic learner

To use your awareness of how you learn best, what you learn from, and the constant opportunities to learn, you need to able to 'switch on' your own natural learner. For some people, this happens automatically – they never lost the delight in learning that they had as children. It is one of the qualities of those who are excellent in their field.

For the rest of us it is necessary to rediscover the natural learner, because it has been stultified by the less than good experiences of learning that we have had.

## switching on your learner

Remember the revised image of the learner we looked at earlier in this chapter? The more you can build this new image in your mind, the more likely you are to regain your natural learner state. To do this, you need to remind yourself of all your own enjoyable experiences of learning – these will push out and replace the old image with its less positive implications.

You can add to this evidence that learning is enjoyable, easy and worthwhile by noticing others who already have the natural learner running automatically. If it works for them, it can work for you too.

*Who do you know of who is a dynamic learner? Use any examples you can think of, including children. Notice the positive effects on them of being a learner, both in terms of the results of their learning and in terms of how they are, their attitude to life.*

## your own learning state

You also need to clarify for yourself how you are when you're switched on to learning. I have talked about triggers in Chapter 5. You now need a trigger for the learning state.

*Think of a specific time when you were enjoying learning. Review in your mind how you were at that moment. Were you relaxed or alert? Leaning forward or back? Physically active or passive? What was your facial expression like? What were you saying to yourself? Really go back into that moment and feel the feeling of being a natural learner. While you are in that moment again, ask yourself, 'What would remind me to automatically be like this whenever I want to?' You will notice that your attention goes to a picture in your mind, or something you could say to yourself, or how you are physically. These are your triggers to regain this state.*

To have this automatically switch on, you need to practise consciously for a while. I always recommend that people do this for certain periods during the week, so that you gently accustom yourself to doing it.

Jane was fed up with boring meetings and resented the amount of time she spent attending them. I proposed to her that she identify a trigger for her learning state, and then switch it on for one meeting out of every two. She tried this out for a while and discovered that she gained more from the meetings where she was switched on. She found after a while that it was 'natural' for her to go to all meetings as a learner. Her boss commented on the change in her attitude and asked her to chair a group undertaking a new project, because she was so good at making meetings more constructive.

## asking the right questions

You can also switch on your learning state by asking yourself the right questions.

Before you engage in an activity ask yourself: 'How can I learn something from this?' After an activity ask yourself: 'What did I usefully learn from this?' (See also the review process under 'Forward thinking' in Chapter 7.)

# learning behaviours

Once you have set yourself up to be a natural learner, you can enhance the process by consciously choosing to adopt the behaviours of a learner.

## look for differences

The learner is always interested in differences, because these are what enable him or her to learn. A new approach, a different point of view, an unexpected reaction – all these create opportunities to learn more. If there are no external stimuli that create difference, then the learner will make his or her own. He or she will ask: 'How else could I tackle this?'

## experiment

Learners try out different approaches to find out which works best. Even if something works quite well, they will still try an alternative, just in case it leads to something better. Obviously not all experiments are successful, but they view this as learning rather than failure. When someone asked Edison what kept him going through so many experiments until he finally created the light-bulb, he said that he had found so many ways not to make a light-bulb, it gradually became obvious! The learner asks: 'I wonder what would happen if I tried this?'

## practice

Learners practise applying their learning so that they become better at it. They do not, however, turn practice into hard work or another way of failing. They make it clear that they are only practising, so that others don't expect them to do it perfectly. In fact, where possible, they get others to encourage them to keep practising. They also give themselves a break from practising, so that it doesn't become a chore.

A manager wanted to experiment with allowing his staff to run their own meetings. He had, up till then, been someone who tightly controlled the meetings and dominated the discussions. He realized that he would find it difficult to let go, so he decided to practise in the meetings with his immediate first-line team. He told them what he wanted to do and asked them to help him by noticing when he succeeded and by gently prompting him when he became too controlling again. When he felt more confident that he could let go of some of the control, he introduced the same process into the first weekly meeting of each month with all his staff.

## make it stimulating

Learners want the learning to be enjoyable, so they create the atmosphere that will support their learning. It is stimulating, in the sense of providing the right stimuli for natural learning.

For some, this means that it is fun, for others that it's stretching or challenging, for others that it is exciting, and for others that it is comfortable and easy. We all have our own preferred combination of these.

The learner recognizes the stimuli that he or she needs, and then asks, 'How can I make this more fun/challenging/exciting/easy?' He or she actively looks for ways to improve the learning opportunity to suit him- or herself.

*Think of something in which you want to develop your learning. Now plan how you can introduce the learning behaviours:*

- *How will you tackle this? And how else could you tackle it?*
- *How can you experiment with approaches?*
- *How will you practise applying your learning? And how will you get encouragement and support in your practice? And how will you pace the practice to keep it enjoyable?*
- *How will you improve the learning process to provide the right stimuli for you?*

It's hard to resist starting right now, isn't it!

# conclusion

Once we become switched on to learning, life is much more interesting! It is a necessity in our rapidly changing world, but it is also a fundamental part of our nature. We thrive on being learners and benefit not only ourselves but others and the world around us. It's not hard work to be a leader in the learning revolution, it's fun!

What is more, we are again modelling one of the important behaviours of the 21st century manager and setting the example for others. We are saying in the clearest way – through our behaviour – that learning is worthwhile and enjoyable; in fact it's the only way to go.

# setting **an example**

So far all the emphasis has been on you and how you relate to yourself. This may seem a bit strange when the role of the manager is geared to managing others. But it is precisely for this reason that I have put so much emphasis on managing yourself.

We can only work with others as well as we work with ourselves. The more I understand about me and what enables me to perform well, the more I will be able to gain the same understanding about others. The better I relate to myself the more able I am to relate to a variety of other people.

There is a second reason for the emphasis on developing your personal qualities: you have more effect on others through how you are than by what you say or do. Whether you like it or not, you are setting an example through your own behaviour and attitudes that others will follow. You are the role model for your staff.

## learning through modelling

The way most of us learn our 'automatic' behaviours and attitudes is through the examples of others in our lives. We start this process in early childhood and at that stage it is fairly obvious. We have all seen children replicate perfectly their parents' behaviour, and probably laughed at it – or groaned if we were the parent and it was not our 'peak performance' they were replicating!

As adults, we continue to absorb others' behaviours and attitudes although not in such an obvious way, because we have already developed our own behaviours and attitudes, so the influence is more subtle. None the less, we tend to take on the behaviours and attitudes of those whom we regard as our 'leaders' in some way, even if it is only while we are in contact with them.

We learn like this because it is easy and natural. We don't think about it, it just happens. How did you learn to be the type of manager you are? Unless you consciously took control of the process, you are probably quite like managers you have had – they are the obvious models – and even if you didn't like everything about their style, there is still a tendency to replicate it.

> I remember being 'educated' about unwritten rules in organizations when I moved to a new job in a community centre. I behaved as I had in my previous job, addressing people by first names, chatting to other staff as I passed their work area, making a cup of coffee when I wanted to. I had noticed that people seemed surprised, but assumed it was because I was new. The deputy called me into his office and said that I was heading for trouble. He said that I needed to behave like everyone else, because the head didn't like familiarity or informality and would come down on me like a ton of bricks if I didn't adjust my behaviour. He told me that if I wanted to survive in the centre, I had better start following the lead of those who had been there a long time and pay attention to how they behaved.

We replicate the behaviour of others as a survival mechanism, to fit in, and after a while it becomes automatic to behave that way.

*Who has influenced your behaviour and attitudes? Notice the different aspects of your way of managing which are very like those of people you have worked for or had close relationships with.*

# being the model

Since you are setting the example for others, you can choose to use this consciously, to create the effect you want. By taking responsibility for ourselves as models, we can begin to exploit the possibilities of this form of learning as an influence on others.

This can seem like an awesome responsibility – after all, we are none of us perfect! But it is surely better to be aware of the example you are setting than to let it happen by default. And it doesn't mean that you have to try to be perfect, it just means that you have to be aware of the example you are setting.

## knowing when to apologize

What people respond to positively is someone who is genuine, who 'walks their talk'. We don't expect perfection from our models, but we do appreciate it if they acknowledge that they too get it wrong sometimes. It is the acknowledgement that matters. This tells us that they are intending to be considerate or patient or whatever, but that they have not yet established it as automatic. Otherwise we wonder if the lack of consideration, etc is really the true nature of the beast!

A manager I knew completely lost his cool one day in the office. He shouted at one of his staff for something they had done, then rounded on the rest and said this was typical of all of them and he was fed up with it. They all scurried away, trying to look busy, and unsure of how to react.

Within the hour, he called a meeting. Everyone went into the room looking very subdued. He said, 'First, I want to publicly apologize to Mick. I had no right to humiliate him like that and I was wrong. Secondly, I want to apologize to all of you. Something had put me in a foul mood this morning and you took the brunt of my mood, instead of what caused it. I know that yelling like that does no good – my old boss used to do it and we really disliked him for it. Underneath all that, there is a grain of truth in what I was yelling about. We do need to do something about the lack of progress in this area, and I'm not sure how to handle it. Can we discuss it? Oh, and will someone put the kettle on – I reckon we all need a cup of coffee!'

His staff were back with him again, and ready to tackle the problem constructively.

Being the model requires that you acknowledge when you're not 'walking the talk'. This does not lose you respect, in fact it increases it.

*When did you last behave in a way that you wish you hadn't? And did you apologize to your staff?*

# being explicit

Sometimes your behaviour makes perfect sense to you – and no sense at all to others. Those who take responsibility for being a model will help others to recognize the model by making it explicit.

Take two examples of managers who want their staff to be more empowered in making decisions.

One just starts saying, 'I don't know, you decide,' when asked for answers by his staff. The staff feel that they are being abandoned, tested, treated unfairly. Far from empowering them, it makes them feel even less sure of their ground.

The other manager calls his staff together and explains to them that he feels that they could make more decisions for themselves without consulting him. He discusses with them how to put this into practice, and they begin to explore possible ways of handing over responsibility and decision-making. The staff feel involved and empowered already.

We cannot assume that others will understand the intentions behind our behaviour. We need to explain our intentions and reasons, to enhance the positive effect of the behaviour.

*Can you think of an example where you behaved in a way that made perfect sense to you but clearly didn't come across that way to your staff? How else could you have handled it?*

## monitoring the effect of your behaviour

If others are reacting in ways you don't intend, as a model you look to your own behaviour as the cause. It is pointless to say, 'They should have . . .' – they didn't, and so you need to try a different tack to elicit the response you want.

In the case of the first manager in the previous example, if he then said, 'Oh well, they're obviously not capable of making decisions,' he would be setting an example of how to give up on something you think is important when you have a setback. Even worse, staff could interpret it as implying that he didn't really want to let them make decisions anyway. Instead, he needs to ask himself, 'How else can I empower my staff to make decisions?' He may even decide to use the second manager as a model!

If you don't know how to improve the effect you are having, you can always try being explicit: 'This is what I intended, but it isn't working. What do I need to do to provoke that response in you?' People are usually very responsive to this sort of direct request for help and, again, it increases their respect for you and models a very constructive behaviour in itself.

# improving the example you set

All the preparatory work of developing yourself, which we have discussed in previous chapters, will automatically develop you as a model for others. There is, however, yet more you can do that will help you to easily improve the example you set.

## using modelling for yourself

Once we become aware of how powerful and easy modelling is as a way of learning, we can use it consciously to develop ourselves. The process is fairly simple:

- *Decide on characteristics you would like to develop further in yourself.* This may be specific skills such as report-writing, or general qualities such as patience.
- *Identify someone who has a characteristic in the form you would like.* This person may be someone you know personally, or someone you know about. It may even be a fictional character, on film or TV.
- *Observe carefully how they are when they demonstrate that characteristic.* Pay particular attention to their physical posture and positioning, their facial expression, their tone of voice.
- *If you know them personally, ask them what they have in their mind just before and while they are demonstrating the characteristic.* This additional information helps you to replicate the state of mind that supports how they are. They may not consciously know this information, but when you ask them they will probably become aware of it.
- *'Try on' being exactly like them when they demonstrate the characteristic.* This mimicry is the first stage of modelling, and best done in private. You adopt their posture, expression and voice tone, and you deliberately put in your mind what they have said they think about.
- *Adjust the mimicry to fit you as a person.* This is a bit like having slight alterations to clothing so that it fits you better. You may find that you are more comfortable if you frown less, sit up straighter, speak slightly more loudly, etc. Experiment with adjustments until the behaviour feels comfortable.
- *Practise the behaviour.* You can now try it out 'in public', remembering that at first you may feel a little strange because you are a learner, so choose safe places to practise until it becomes integrated for you.

*Choose a characteristic you would like to develop and find a model for yourself. Go through this process.*

You may have noticed that I don't suggest that you copy their words. Although the way they express themselves may be useful, we can be misled into thinking that if we say the same thing we will have the same effect. In fact, it is the rest of their communication, through their body and voice tone, that has the most impact, so it is this that I suggest you concentrate on when practising modelling. It is also those aspects of someone's behaviour that we pick up in unconscious modelling – the things that convey the intention and attitude behind the words.

By choosing to consciously model those who already have the characteristics we wish to develop, we reduce the risk of unconsciously modelling behaviours that are less useful.

## our heroes

Most of us have people or characters we admire and respect. These are in fact models we have already chosen at an unconscious level. They have certain characteristics we aspire to. Here are some examples:

| *Hero* | *Characteristics* |
|---|---|
| Bob Dylan | Constantly evolving, creative, time to himself, inspirational with words |
| Indiana Jones | Adventurous, believes he can succeed no matter what the odds |
| Anita Roddick | Ethical, concerned about the environment, successful businesswoman, has fun, lively, enjoys her work |
| Billy Connolly | Funny, genuine, loves the countryside, doesn't accept bullshit |

*Who are some of your heroes? List them and the characteristic(s) they have that you admire. They may be fictional or real people, alive or dead, famous or not well-known. Notice that you only list the characteristics you admire – they may have other characteristics that you don't want, and that's fine – you don't have to take on the whole person.*

Do not underestimate the importance of your heroes. They offer you a rich source of models and exposure to them allows you to unconsciously pick up more of those characteristics.

So if you have a favourite film with a character who is a hero, watch it as often as you can – it helps your development in the most enjoyable way! Or read the biography again, watch the documentary, listen to the tape – whenever you can remind yourself of your heroes, do.

## allies

We can also use these same characters, or others, as our 'invisible allies'. When we are trying out new behaviours and approaches, we can feel quite vulnerable and are often unsure of exactly how to react.

It is very useful to have a source of support and advice when we feel like this, and your 'invisible allies' can provide this. This may sound really strange to you, but stop and think about it for a moment. Human beings have always done this, in different ways. Some cultures believe that the spirits of animals and ancestors are with them, supporting them. Children often have 'invisible friends', and many of us call on God or guardian angels when we're not sure what to do! This is the equivalent, used consciously to help us.

> Jenny confided to me that when she did a presentation, she imagined that her dad was at her side, which gave her confidence, because he had always encouraged and supported her.
>
> Jack, on the other hand, didn't believe in such fantasizing. He did admit, however, that when he had a situation where he wasn't sure how to react, he would think to himself, 'Well, what would John Harvey-Jones do now?' He found that this was a useful way of sorting out how he should react.

These are two good examples of how to use allies to support you in your development.

*How could you use invisible allies to support you? And who would you choose? List four examples of your own.*

## conclusion

You have more influence on others by the example you set than by any other means. Every step forward you take in your development will increase the positive effect you have on others.

It is up to you to use the power of modelling positively and consciously, and to remember that you can use the same method to enhance your own development. Make sure the influences on you are positive and useful ones by choosing them consciously.

By recognizing yourself as being a model for others, you can take control of the example you set, and by using modelling to improve yourself you are again demonstrating to your staff the importance of continual learning.

# endpiece

## and if it's hard to transform yourself

Once you begin to work on yourself you may find that you spend more time noticing how you are failing than how you are making progress. We all 'fall from grace' and once we are aware of the way we could be, we are also more aware of how often we don't match up to that ideal. I would suggest several things to help you when you experience this:

- *Let yourself off.* Don't berate yourself for not being how you want to be. It is an ideal and you are human – allow for your human-ness. Give yourself a day off from even trying, then start again.
- *Read.* Take something from the reading list at the back of this book and get some fresh inspiration.
- *Give yourself some treats.* Help yourself get into a better state. After all, you are now aware of where you don't match up to your ideal. Before, you probably wouldn't even have noticed, so you deserve a reward.
- *Count your successes.* We often notice what we haven't done and overlook what we *have* achieved. Make a list of the times when you have matched up to your ideal.

Our development is not in a straight line. We tend to go round and round the same spirals, but each time we are moving further forwards, so don't give up. This is a lifelong task and you may as well enjoy the journey.

# Communicating Effectively

Part II concentrated on your self-development, to build a strong model for others to follow. We have looked at most of the characteristics of an effective leader, listed in Chapter 2.

The one characteristic we haven't considered yet is communicating well. This covers so many different things that I am devoting Part III to looking at the major factors of communication that are crucial to your effectiveness as a 21st century manager.

# building **rapport**

When we think of communication we tend to think of saying or writing things, and wonder what words we should use. But communication begins with the way we relate to others. The messages we give about how we feel about others are the underpinning of our verbal communications with them. If I don't think that you like or respect me, I will not take in what you are saying to me, even if it is important or useful.

We cannot artificially create rapport. It is the natural result of feeling that there is a positive relationship between us. We can, however, be conscious of the elements that contribute to building rapport and choose to use them positively to make a difference to our communication.

## why bother?

It is important to begin by considering what makes it worth your while to build rapport with others. To many, taking the time to form relationships is wasting a scarce resource – your time. You need to be convinced that the pay-offs from rapport are sufficient to make it a valuable area in which to make an effort. The most convincing evidence you will find will be in your own experience.

> Martin was not convinced that good relationships mattered. He thought that his main responsibilities were to get the work done in time and to ensure that his staff had clear instructions on how to fulfil their part of the job.
>
> I asked him whom he had done his best work for. He immediately named a boss he had had in a different company. I asked him what she was like. He used words like approachable, interested, supportive, and described both her and his work there with enthusiasm and affection.
>
> I didn't have to ask him to draw the obvious conclusions – he had convinced himself.

*What benefits can you think of that would result from enhancing your rapport with others? Come up with at least five.*

Having convinced ourselves it's worthwhile building rapport, we now need to consider the elements that enable us to do so automatically.

# your intention

Often we don't think about our overall intention in our contact with people. If we neglect to consciously consider our intention, we will none the less convey some sort of intention to them, and frequently this will be negative.

Comments about managers I have heard include:

- 'She doesn't value me for what I do.'
- 'I'm just another link in the chain to him.'
- 'She's condescending towards us.'
- 'He only cares about getting the job done.'

The fact that you didn't mean to convey that impression is irrelevant – that is how they think you feel towards them, because they don't have any positive message of intention.

## how to clarify your intention

Your overall intention is how you want to come across to others in your dealings with them. It governs your attitude towards them, and will colour all your interactions. Because your attitude to others affects strongly their reaction to you, it is important to consider it carefully.

### your beliefs about others

You begin by considering your beliefs about other people. This underlies your attitude towards others.

- Do you think most people are likeable?
- Are most people awkward to deal with?
- Do you look forward to meeting new people?
- Do you prefer to stick to your own circle of friends?
- Do you think people are often stupid?
- Do you expect hostility?
- Do you care about how people react to you?

*What are your answers to these questions?*

As you begin to consider these questions, you will realize that you do have strong beliefs about others, as a generalization. The question to then ask yourself is not if you are right or wrong, but rather: 'Is it useful to me to have this belief about others?' You can find evidence to support any belief – if you couldn't, it wouldn't be a belief! So what you need to do is to select beliefs about people that have the effect you want and make sure you collect evidence to support these beliefs.

*What would be a useful set of beliefs about others that would help you to have a positive intention towards them? Here are some examples:*

■ *People have something to contribute.*
■ *People are generally friendly and helpful.*

*Write down your own list. Now consider what evidence you have in your experience that supports these beliefs.*

## your attitude

Linked to your beliefs about others is the attitude you approach them with:

■ What do you want to convey to them about how you feel about them?
■ How do you want them to react to you?

By clarifying in your own mind how you want the interaction to go, as opposed to just what you want to say, you enhance the likelihood of having that effect. Our unconscious mind tends to direct our behaviour. If you have a clear intention to form a positive relationship, you will tend to automatically behave and speak in a way that makes it possible.

*Write down a description of the attitude you would like to approach people with, answering the two questions above. Now read it over to yourself, out loud if possible, to confirm it to your unconscious.*

By consciously choosing to have useful beliefs and a positive attitude towards others, we set ourselves up to have a much better chance of establishing good relationships. After all, we tend to get what we expect – have you noticed? This is sometimes called 'a self-fulfilling prophecy'. If I expect someone to be awkward, they usually are! If, on the other hand, I give myself a positive intention, and expect others to respond positively, they usually do!

## your state

In Chapter 5 I stressed the point that how you are in yourself affects everything you do. When building rapport, you need to begin by ensuring that you are in a positive state yourself. We cannot relate well to others if we are not relating well to ourselves.

You can use the techniques I proposed in Chapter 5 for resourcing yourself. It is also helpful to spend a couple of minutes before interacting with others in remembering some specific situations where you gained support from others easily and successfully. This helps to give you the mind-set to repeat the process automatically.

*Think of two examples now. Recall how you were, physically and mentally. Remember how the other person reacted, and relive the enjoyment of being in rapport with somebody.*

## your outcomes

When we think beforehand about our interactions with others, we tend to concentrate on the result we want out of the interaction:

- 'I want them to agree to do x.'
- 'I want us to find a way to achieve y.'
- 'I want them to know about z.'

This is important, but it is not the only outcome we want. We also want a particular effect:

- 'I want them to agree willingly.'
- 'I want them to contribute ideas on how to achieve y.'
- 'I want them to want to act on z.'

Getting to the effects we want will depend on whether we establish a good relationship with them. If we consciously consider the effect we want, we will make it more likely that we behave in ways that enhance the relationship and don't just communicate in a task-driven way.

There is also a longer-term outcome. If we are continually building rapport and enhancing relationships through our interactions with others, our contact with them becomes easier and easier. Sometimes it is more important to build relationships than to get the immediate result.

James had just returned from a first meeting with a potential new customer. When he walked in, Sue asked him how he had got on. He said he was sorry, but he had failed to get an order, then added: 'But I did get on famously with Mr Bryan, and he asked me join him for a drink after work, to talk more about our shared passion for Mozart's music. And I feel quite comfortable about asking for another meeting in a week or two, and I'm sure we'll end up with an order.' Sue congratulated him on a successful meeting.

*Think about a particular meeting you have coming up. Consider what results you want, and what effect you want the meeting to have on the individuals concerned. Also consider the longer-term effects you want: how do you want it to be when you have contact with that person again?*

# finding the right level

Once you begin an interaction with the person, you can add to the rapport-building that will occur as a result of your preparatory thinking on beliefs, attitudes and outcomes. You do this by switching on your awareness.

## assessing the mood

We often launch straight into a conversation with someone without taking a moment to consider what is happening with them. This certainly doesn't build rapport, and sometimes will break existing rapport.

Hazel was excited about receiving approval for a major project. She rushed straight over to James's office to tell him about it. She knew they got on well, so didn't consider it necessary to stop and think about their interaction.

She arrived in his office and launched straight in to telling him about the decision and asked him when he thought they could get started. When she finally registered that James was very quiet and unresponsive it was too late.

He had heard that morning that two of his friends had been made redundant. He was sad for them and it had made him feel uncertain about his own future. He couldn't believe how insensitive Hazel was and felt quite distanced from her.

It only takes a moment to stop and notice how the other person is. We can then adjust our behaviour to be more 'in tune' with them. This doesn't mean that if someone is depressed, we should become depressed too. That would be taking rapport to a level that isn't useful! It *does* mean:

- If they are speaking quietly, use a gentle tone.
- If they are sitting still, be still physically.
- If they are relaxed, release your own physical tension.
- If they are thoughtful, slow down your speech and gestures.
  (And, of course, the opposites.)

This is what we do automatically when we have genuine rapport with someone. We pick up their mood and behave in a complementary way. Just stopping for a moment and taking notice is often enough to switch on a matching manner automatically. The difference in the effect we have on the other person is remarkable. They feel that we are 'on their wavelength' and are much more likely to respond positively to us.

*Think about some of your colleagues. Choose three and take recent examples of your interactions with them. Did you adjust your behaviour to complement their mood?*

*Now take one example where you didn't. How would you adjust your behaviour if you were to replay this scenario? How would you adjust your expectations?*

# the right language

As a manager, you are likely to need to know several languages. I don't mean 'foreign' languages; I mean that different groups you work with will have different ways of expressing themselves. Before you start your conversation, you need to take a moment to remember which language to use, which way to express yourself.

Doctors are renowned for describing illnesses in terms that no layperson can understand. We don't even know which part of our body they are talking about, let alone what's really wrong, or what the implications are for us. Some managers are similar.

In any organization, there is likely to be:

- company-speak;
- manager-speak;
- technical-speak;
- down-to-earth practical-speak;

- customer-speak;
- supplier-speak.

An excellent manager 'translates' from one of these to the other when conveying messages.

> Dave had been to a senior managers' meeting where they had discussed the proposed quality initiatives and concluded that his area would pilot the new recording system to understand variations in the process. He met with his team and gave them the news by saying: 'OK folks, I've volunteered us to try out an experiment. We're going to keep a note of what goes right and what goes wrong in our bit of the process, to see if we can identify the underlying cause of problems instead of leaping in and fire-fighting. It'll mean a bit of extra work in the short term, but should save us some of the reworking we normally have to do in the longer term.'
>
> He went on to give more detail, but he already had his team with him. He was 'talking their language'.

In this 'translation', the manager had moved from receiving a message to interpreting that message and translating it into the language his team would pick up on straight away. Not only did it enable him to get his message across more effectively, it also reinforced the team's relationship with him.

It sounds like a complicated process, doesn't it? But in reality, you often do it automatically. Just by thinking about what will make sense to the other person, you switch on your 'translator'. And they feel more at ease and comfortable with you because you talk their language.

## acknowledging difference

Finding the right level is all about acknowledging the individuality of the person you're addressing. It simply requires us to notice how they are, rather than assume that our way will automatically suit them. (We will look in more detail at noticing difference in Chapter 13 on influencing.)

# valuing people

Rapport is established when you clearly value people. All we have looked at in this chapter is about setting yourself up to have an automatic valuing of others, so that they receive that message. Some people, however, will resist and continue to be difficult to relate to.

## building trust

In these cases, you need to be prepared to build up trust over a period of time. This reminds us that building rapport is not a one-off activity. It requires a consistent approach to others.

Rapport is established by your general manner towards others, and can easily be broken by evidence that you are not consistent. It is not enough to find the right level with someone when you have something important to convey to them. Their relationship with you will be affected by:

- you greeting them pleasantly in the morning;
- you remembering they were off ill last week and asking them if they're better;
- the way they see you treat others;
- your active interest in the work they're doing.

You have to be constantly demonstrating that you are someone who treats building rapport as a priority. Otherwise it may seem like manipulation.

> I remember a telling comment from a staff member about the new director: 'Our old boss was only nice to you if he wanted you to do something. This guy is friendly and considerate even when it doesn't matter. I've never seen him put anyone down, or talk over their head. He seems to genuinely care.'

## the dangers of relating well

Some managers fear that if they are too 'friendly' with their staff they will lose respect and control. I would suggest that there is a difference between rapport and collusion that needs to be clarified here.

Rapport is friendly respect for another, which elicits a similar response in them. Collusion is playing along with others to make them feel you're on their side, even if that compromises your integrity. I believe that most managers know the difference and can establish rapport rather than collusion.

*Think about your own examples of having rapport with others, in particular your own line managers. Did it mean that you didn't respect them, didn't work well for them?*

There is far more danger in distancing yourself from people. Unless they feel comfortable with you and feel that you value them as individuals, they will not respond constructively and positively to you. You will be constantly trying to counteract their negative reactions.

## conclusion

Building rapport with others is vital to communicating effectively. You cannot force people into rapport with you, but you can develop an attitude that makes it more likely that you will have rapport. And if your behaviour with others shows consideration and respect, then you will automatically find you have more rapport.

This underpins all the rest of your communication. The pay-offs are enormous. And your life at work is easier and more enjoyable. How can you resist putting this development as a priority?

# giving **and receiving information**

I have always liked the simple reminder: 'We were given two ears and one mouth – use them in that ratio!' We tend to think of communicating as talking, but we communicate just as much, if not more, when we are listening. So we will start this chapter by looking at how we receive information.

## receiving information

The manager who is open to receiving information is the manager who is aware of current reality in the workplace. He or she is also able to counteract problems before they grow into crises, because he or she sees the early warning signals. You will also find that staff trust these managers and take notice of them. The pay-offs are useful!

Excellence in receiving information consists of three factors:

1. Wanting to be informed.
2. Paying attention.
3. Using information well.

## wanting to be informed

The first step, as you might expect, is to have the mind-set that is interested and curious about what is going on. We need to be convinced that it is in our best interests to be open to receiving information from others. I gave some of the pay-offs in the previous paragraph.

If we have successfully switched on our natural learner we will already be open to receiving information, because the natural learner knows that others are a very valuable source of our own learning and development.

It is not enough to think that it's a 'good thing' to tell people, 'I want you to tell me about everything,' or 'I want you to be open with me.' Unless you are convinced emotionally as well as intellectually that it's worthwhile for you, your behaviour will betray you and people will stop keeping you informed. So what will convince you, if you are not already convinced?

*First, think of your own list of pay-offs for being open to receiving information. Now think of some examples when you have been open to receiving information from others and found it beneficial. Really re-experience the moment and remember how valuable it was for you to be informed. Begin to build your evidence that it's worth your while.*

## paying attention

Once you are open to receiving information, you need to check out the way you receive information. Most of us have learned to be very selective and judgemental listeners. We 'switch off' if we don't think it has any relevance to us and when we do listen we are constantly judging the information or the person.

---

Jim was telling his manager about the problems with his current project. The manager already thought Jim was not up to scratch, and as she listened to his story she was thinking, 'Typical of him, to have problems. He probably didn't plan it properly. And he expects me to get him off the hook with the customer – no way!'

Jim then said: 'So what do you think I should do about the proposed change in the outcome?' His manager was thrown. 'What proposed change?' she asked. 'I've just told you that in the last review session with the customer, he asked if I would increase the flexibility of the program to include some extra linked database capacity.'

She hadn't been listening properly. He was doing a better job than she had expected. Unfortunately, Jim had already given up his hope that this time she might actually pay attention.

---

There is no doubt that it is sometimes useful to be selective in your listening. We couldn't possibly absorb all the information that is thrown at us, and much of it may be irrelevant to us. However, if you have the 'filters' on all the time, you miss out on important things and also lose the trust and openness of your staff, because they 'sense' that you are judging and not giving them your full attention.

When we do pay attention, it is often still equated with listening to all the words. The 'proof' that we have paid attention is that we can repeat verbatim what was said. Most of us learned at school that this is what paying attention means, when some teacher challenged us to repeat back to them what they said, or at exam time when you had to regurgitate the notes made in class. However, this is really only superficial attention. True attention is at five levels:

1. Listening to the words, so you know what is being said.
2. Listening to the meaning behind the words, the nuances, emphases, hesitations, etc.
3. Noticing with your eyes how the body language adds to the meaning of the words.
4. Using your intuition – your 'gut reaction' – to read between the lines.
5. Keeping your heart in touch with what's going on, so that you have empathy with the person concerned.

True attention is very powerful:

- It enables you to hear the full story and thus react more appropriately.
- It gives you extra information about how this person ticks and what really matters to them.
- It means that the other person feels valued and listened to, and increases your rapport with that person.

When you give this type of attention you have no space to make judgements as the person is talking: you're too busy paying attention. This means that you have the full story before you begin reacting and so are able to draw more useful conclusions. It also means that the message you give off to the speaker is more useful. People will sense if you are giving them full attention and will respond to this by being more open and detailed in their information.

This form of attention-giving is not completely alien to us, and most of us have done it sometimes. Babies often get this form of attention, because they cannot confuse us with words! And parents are remarkably good at understanding babies' communication.

*When have you given this true attention to others? It may be close friends, or someone you found interesting or attractive. Think about the effect on you and them of this form of attention. You may also think of the times when someone has given you this form of attention. Notice how much more willing we are to open up, and how much more comfortable we feel with someone who is paying full attention. You could also notice how you look when you are giving full attention, how you sit or stand, etc, so that you know what full attention is like physically, as well as emotionally. (Remember that you can use your own best practice as an example.)*

## what if the information you are receiving is not relevant?

If you are paying full attention, you will notice very quickly if the information seems to you to be irrelevant. Rather than just switch off, it is more useful to check with the person concerned how they think this relates to the subject. Don't do this with a sharp question like: 'What's this got to do with what we're talking about?' People will sense the judgement, and clam up. If you simply and gently ask: 'And how does this relate to what we're talking about?' it prompts the person to either explain how they believe it's relevant, or to acknowledge that they have gone off on a tangent, without feeling too bad about it. After all, the question is proof that you were paying attention.

I am not advocating that you constantly give others your full attention. You would quickly wear yourself out if you did. However, it is worth your while to give this level of attention when receiving important information, and sometimes just to allow yourself to get to know more about the person.

---

Asking people to give this level of attention to each other is an activity I use a lot in my training work. They are not exchanging important information, just telling personal stories to each other. Besides gaining practice in giving attention, there is almost always the added benefit of feeling more 'in tune' with the other person. In fact, I usually have difficulty in getting them to stop their interaction.

---

## using information well

Once we have received information, it is important that we use it well. All information has some purpose, and until it is used for that purpose it is not useful information. (The only exception to this is malicious information – gossip, or telling tales about colleagues. In this instance, good use of the information may be to refuse to listen to it!)

When people have given us information, they want some proof that we have used it well. Sometimes they will have this proof by your immediate reaction. If you have clearly understood their explanation or position, and you show this by your response, then they will feel able to talk to you openly again.

If the information requires some action and you take that action, then again, they will know you have used the information well. Notice that sometimes they will not automatically know that you have taken the action, and you may need to tell them.

Syd was complaining to me that he had discussed with his manager the possibility of attending a management diploma course and he had thought that his manager was very sympathetic to his cause. He had left the details with his manager 10 days before, for him to add his endorsement before it went to the training department. Since then, he had heard nothing. 'So I guess he wasn't that supportive after all.' I suggested he went and asked his manager. The next day I saw him again. He was over the moon. 'He said that he had endorsed it and sent it straight through to training. They had said that they would let him have final approval by next Wednesday, so he was waiting for that before he told me. I wish he had said. I was beginning to think that I'd wasted my breath with him.'

If the information is only to keep you up to date on something, or helping to clarify details of some ongoing task, then you just need to acknowledge its usefulness to you. And do remember to refer to it the next time you meet that person. It so pleases people when you say, 'How did x go last week?' or 'How far along are you with y now?' They know that you really did pay attention if you remember it some time later.

If the information is sensitive or confidential, then it is vital that you do not repeat it or use it inappropriately. It is very important to check with people if you are not sure whether the information falls into this category. For example, someone may tell you that they are thinking about applying for a new job. Some people will already have told their colleagues and be glad to discuss it openly. Others may wish the information to be kept under wraps for now. Don't assume which of these applies; ask.

*How good are you at receiving information? Consider two examples from your recent experience: one where you did it well – and notice how you did it; one where it could have been better – ask yourself what improvements you would make next time.*

# asking for information

In order to have an overview, and to keep abreast of what is going on, you are likely to ask for information from your staff. When you ask for information, you need to consider two factors:

- Exactly what information you want.
- What the information is for.

# exactly what information you want

It is important to clarify exactly what you want, because otherwise you may receive a lot of information that is irrelevant to you.

A manager who had just taken over a team told them that he wanted to be kept informed about what was happening on their projects. Within a fortnight he was regretting the statement. He was receiving reports, verbal and written, about all the day-to-day details, and the staff were consulting him on their every decision.

At the next meeting he apologized to them for his lack of clarity, and said that what he really wanted was a fortnightly update that kept him informed about whether they were on schedule, any major developments, any major problems, and which gave them a chance to ask any questions they had or to raise any issues. He suggested that this be a verbal report, and that they should schedule regular one-hour slots in his diary. He added that if it only took half an hour, that was fine.

When you ask your staff to tell you about something, you need to clarify what exactly you want to know so that they can offer you the information you need in the form you prefer. There is much custom and practice in the area of information that is not useful. In particular, there is too much written reporting that is just filed away. This is definitely a leftover from the control style of management where the manager wants proof that he or she can refer back to, but actually doesn't really take notice of what it says at the time. This takes up time and energy for both you and your staff which could be better used in a different way.

*Before your next team meeting, stop and think about what information you really want and clarify that with your staff beforehand.*

# what the information is for

Closely linked to the point about exactly what information you want is the question of what the information is for. There is a lot of difference between the type of information we need to stay aware of what is going on and the type of information we need to put in an annual report. By considering how the information is to be used, we make it easier for the other person to make it useful and relevant. We also make it clear to them how they will have proof that we have used the information well, because its purpose has already been stated. Further, we make it easier for ourselves to receive the information well, because it will be more likely to fit our requirements.

'I want to know what you are doing next week, to see if we can schedule a half-day together' will elicit a different response from 'I want to know what you are doing next week, because I'm trying to get a sense of what takes up most of your time.' And if we just ask 'I want to know what you are doing next week,' staff are left wondering what to tell you about.

This clarity in your requests for information makes life easier for both you and your staff and avoids a lot of misunderstanding.

*When you ask for information, do you clarify your reasons for asking for it? Consider how you could improve on the clarification you already give.*

# giving information

Many of the points I have made about receiving and asking for information apply equally to giving information. There tend to be two basic trends in giving information:

- On a 'need-to-know' basis, decided by the manager.
- Giving all the information possible, creating overload.

## 'need-to-know' information

This is often used as a means of creating a power base for the manager, by restricting the information given to staff. By deciding for them what will be important for them to know, you take away their right to decide for themselves what is relevant and useful.

## all information

When you give staff all the information you have, you are in danger of overloading them. They then end up not listening to any of the information and missing those parts that are most relevant to them.

## giving appropriate information

There is a balance to be achieved between these two extremes. This requires that you act as a 'translator' (I referred to this in the last chapter). It is important that staff know what information is available, so that they can decide if they need to know more. However, you need to filter the information you give to ensure that it is useful.

## the purpose of the information

There are a number of reasons for giving information, such as:

■ to let staff know that they can find out more if they want to;
■ to let them know about organizational issues that may affect them (this needs to have its relevance pointed out);
■ to prompt them into action (this needs the action required made clear);
■ to ask them for their views (the fact that this is what you want needs to be made explicit);
■ to give them feedback (this needs to refer to the information they gave you, so that they recognize the link).

By clarifying the purpose of the information you are giving, you:

■ make it easier for yourself to present the information appropriately;
■ make it easier for your staff to receive and respond to the information appropriately.

## the relevance of the information

When you give information, you need to ensure that it is presented in a way that makes its relevance clear to your staff. This may require you to 'translate' the information from concepts into action, or you may have to link the information to your everyday practice: 'What this means for us is that . . .'

## the format of the information

When you have considered the purpose and relevance of the information, you can more easily decide on the appropriate way of presenting it.

Many meetings are lengthened significantly by people giving information verbally that would have been better received if written down as main points to be discussed or clarified, and circulated beforehand. And many written documents are full of information that people do not need to remember in detail – they just need the action points.

I remember discussing the 'failure' of team briefings with a manager. She was concerned that, although she kept her team fully informed by repeating almost verbatim the information given to her in her team briefings, they didn't seem to remember it, they didn't ask questions, and they just wanted to finish the meeting as soon as possible.

Before the next team briefing we went through together what she wanted to cover. At each point, I asked her to consider the purpose and relevance of the information for her team, and then how she could best present it. After a few such exercises, she reported back that team briefings were going much better. One of her staff suggested to me that maybe their manager had finally realized that most of the briefings she received herself were boring, and had stopped just repeating them verbatim. 'We now feel that the briefings are useful to us, instead of her just doing what she's supposed to by reporting back to us.'

*Consider your next team briefing or its equivalent.*

■   *Why are you giving them the information?*
■   *What response do you want to the information?*
■   *How will you make it relevant?*
■   *How can you best present it?*

By improving the way in which you give information, you significantly affect the response you get from your staff.

# feedback

A specific form of information you will be both giving and receiving is feedback. Feedback is used here in the sense of reactions and responses to particular behaviours or actions.

## receiving feedback

For the 21st century manager who is developing his or her skills and attitudes, receiving feedback from others is vital. You need to know if your behaviour is having the effect you want, in order to establish what is working and what still needs to be developed. You can do this in several ways:

- formal feedback processes;
- asking for informal feedback;
- paying careful attention to reactions.

## formal feedback processes

Many organizations have now introduced 360-degree feedback. This usually takes the form of a questionnaire on the manager's behaviour and style of management, which is issued to some of their direct reports, their peers and their own line manager. The results of the questionnaire are then collated and form the basis for discussion between the manager and either the line manager or the human resources representative. There is also a discussion with the team about their feedback to the manager.

This can be very valuable if used well, as it gives a variety of perspectives on the manager and enables him or her to see how he or she comes across to the different groups.

Mike was engaged in a leadership development programme and was asked to use the 360-degree appraisal process to help him to assess his progress.

He was surprised and pleased to find that his staff had noticed positive changes in his style, and were now rating him more highly on such skills as listening and involving others. To his disappointment, his own boss did not seem to have noticed any positive changes – her assessment of him was very similar to the previous one, except that her rating of his organizational skills was lower. Mike felt that this was unfair and wanted to defend himself. His peers who were also on the programme had noticed more changes than those who weren't.

When the results were discussed in the next stage of the programme, he realized that it was all useful information on the effect he was having on others. While his staff were definitely noticing improvements, as were his peers who shared his experience of the development programme, his development had not yet reached the point of being effective in influencing his peers, or affecting positively his boss's view. He needed to explore how he could begin to apply the principles he was learning to his sideways and upwards relationships as well.

*Using formal feedback well.* It is important that you learn to accept feedback as useful information rather than react to it. This is particularly important when you meet with your team to discuss their feedback. If you are not having the effect on others you want to have, you need to think of different ways of getting that message across, or providing evidence that they will react to positively.

You may need to ask the person concerned for examples of what would cause them to revise their view of you in a particular category, so that you know what sort of behaviours would make the difference. It can also be useful to find out what exactly you did that caused someone to rate you more highly so that you know what specific behaviours are having a positive effect.

By asking for examples, you not only increase the usefulness of the information to you but also make it clear that you do want to use the feedback, which encourages others to give you more, and in constructive ways.

## asking for informal feedback

The drawback to formal feedback processes is that they tend to be infrequent and only give a general picture. Sometimes you will find it useful to ask for feedback about a specific situation or behaviour, so that you can check out whether it has been effective or not.

---

Susan had decided to revise the way in which she ran her team meetings. She produced a briefing paper on what she wanted to do and the intended end result, and revised the usual agenda to conform to the new formula. She asked for any comments before the meeting to be sent to her – none were forthcoming.

She therefore went ahead with the next meeting according to the new formula and at the end of the meeting asked staff to evaluate the effect of the revised approach. The staff had appreciated what she was trying to do, and offered constructive comments about what worked and what still needed to be revised. She found their feedback most useful.

---

*Using informal feedback well.*   It is important to think about your questions when asking for feedback. If you just say, 'What did you think of that?' people will tend to give you either neutral and generalized comments, such as, 'It was all right,' or to be critical: 'I didn't like the way you . . .' This is not useful information.

I would suggest that you ask specific questions for feedback: 'What went well in that?' or 'What did you like about that?' These questions will tell you what worked, and give you answers that are much more effective than 'It was all right.' Then you should ask, 'What would you have liked to have been different and how?', 'How could I change it to improve it?' These questions give you constructive information about amending your approach or behaviour, rather than a general criticism.

## paying careful attention to reactions

There is always feedback available to us. People react, both verbally and non-verbally, to everything we do. When you don't get the reaction you want, it is important to take responsibility for that. Often we want to blame the other person: 'They misunderstood me' or 'They didn't get it.' Much more useful is to learn that that approach didn't work and to try a different one.

*Using reactions well.* Most of us notice reactions – especially negative ones – even if we don't admit it. Use that information! But first check out if it really is a negative reaction to your behaviour or communication. Sometimes the negative reaction is for other reasons.

> I had phoned someone to ask what was happening with a particular project. He was very short with me and asked if he could ring back later. I wondered if I had said something wrong.
>
> When he did ring back later on, I asked if I had upset him in some way. He apologized and said that he was already late for a meeting when I rang, so hadn't time to talk. We had a useful conversation, and I was glad that I hadn't just assumed that I had upset him and reacted accordingly.

Also, don't forget that if you get a positive reaction, it can sometimes be worth checking out why. This will tell you what made the difference, so you can use it again.

## unsolicited feedback

Sometimes people give you feedback without being asked. I must admit that my heart sinks a little when someone says, 'Can I give you some feedback on this?' as it nearly always turns out to be critical. It seems to be automatic for us to tell people what we don't like rather than what we like or appreciate about their behaviour.

However, we can learn to control our own reaction to this and turn it into useful information. First I suggest you listen respectfully to the person's view. Secondly, ask them how they would suggest it could be improved. Finally, ask them if there were any parts of it that were useful to them, or that they liked. Through this process we gain more useful information, and others are beginning to learn how to give feedback constructively.

*In the next few days, actively take the opportunity to receive feedback. Remember to ask for positive feedback as well as criticism, and if someone is critical, ask them how things could be improved.*

Receiving feedback is not easy. We are well trained to be defensive or to try and ignore the implications of negative feedback. And we tend not to notice or to be embarrassed by positive feedback. However, once you become an active seeker of feedback, you will find that it is a most useful tool for self-development, and that others improve the way they offer it to you.

# giving feedback

Just as you can gain from the feedback others give to you, so you can help others to develop themselves by giving feedback constructively. The rule here is simple: *give feedback in the way you would find it useful to receive feedback.*

## giving positive feedback

So often we don't think to tell people the positive things we notice. Yet when we do, it makes them feel valued and also encourages them to do more of what we are valuing.

It doesn't have to be a major event, nor does it need to be fulsome praise. In fact, praising someone for something ordinary can come across as condescension. However, noticing that they did it, or saying thank you, can make a lot of difference.

> I was talking to Robert, an administrative assistant in a management team. He had not been in the post long, and I asked him how he found the job.
>
> 'I'm working very hard and I love it,' he said. He went on to say that this was the first time he had worked in a team where he felt that his contribution was really valued. When I asked him what gave him that impression, he said: 'Everyone here says please and thank you. They always check whether you can fit in the job they're asking you to do for them, and accept it if you say you can't, because they trust you to know the priorities. I go to team meetings, and am asked to contribute views and ideas, not just take the notes. And my part in getting a task achieved is always acknowledged.'
>
> Robert went on to study in his own time for qualifications in his particular field of work and became a project manager in the team some two years later.

It's up to you as the team leader to set the example of actively giving positive feedback to team members, so that it becomes an everyday habit.

## constructive feedback

When things aren't going according to plan, it's easy to get into the 'blame culture'. But telling someone that they have made a mistake or not come up to scratch is not helpful in avoiding the problem recurring. This doesn't mean that you should say nothing: it means that you need to help them to learn from the mistake, or work out ways to improve their performance.

Dwelling on what went wrong doesn't help anyone, as we have all experienced. It is up to you to turn around the situation, and you can do this by either giving suggestions as to what would improve the results, or by asking the person concerned what they think would make a difference next time. It is also important to check out that mistakes have been learned from, by both the person concerned and by others.

A group I work with are actively engaged in helping to move their company into the 21st century in its use of technology. They realized that they were avoiding an important part of what was happening in their work. Things often didn't work out, and they were falling into the 'old' habit of trying to hide or excuse themselves when things went wrong.

They decided to tackle this differently, and they now have mistakes as a regular item on their team meeting agenda. Everyone brings something they haven't done well to the table and explains what went wrong, what they have learned, and what action they are taking to rectify it.

It is considered to be one of the most useful items on the agenda, for both individual and team development.

*How do you and your team deal with mistakes? Could you improve it so that mistakes are valued?*

## feedback on action

The final area of feedback worth mentioning again is that of telling people what has happened as a result of information they have given to you. We need to know that our information has been used or acted upon, if we are to continue to want to give information. Sometimes the final result is some way off, or outside our area, and we want to know that we have had an effect.

Sam had written up a report on his team's customer survey, as part of the material to be reported to the board.

He commented to me several weeks later that he didn't even know if it was incorporated in the final report, yet alone how the board had reacted to it. He had put a lot of time and effort into improving the survey, and wanted to know that it had been worthwhile. His fear was that the lack of feedback meant that it wasn't considered important or valuable. His resentment was that no one had bothered to mention it again.

It is simple enough to tell people what you have done as a result of their information. Even telling them that nothing has happened yet is useful, because it gives them the message that you are aware of it, and do care.

*Look at how you give feedback in all three categories:*

1.  *Decide to give some unsolicited positive feedback to every member of your team in the next week.*
2.  *Turn a mistake or poor performance into a constructive learning experience.*
3.  *Who have you forgotten to give a progress report to? Tell them what you have done with their information.*

## conclusion

Information is central to the effective working of a team. You have the responsibility of setting the example for how information is given and received. By improving the way in which you use information, you will set the ground rules for how information is transmitted and used throughout your team.

The most commonly mentioned area for improvement in managers' skills is 'communication'. When you ask people what they really mean by this, you will find that it is based on the lack of skill in giving and receiving information.

We are now in a period where information is crucial in all businesses. Learning to handle this area well is vital to the 21st century manager.

# setting a direction

There are some leaders who are renowned for inspiring others with their vision, such as Ghandi and his vision of independence for India, and Mandela with his vision for a new South Africa. These may seem like lofty examples, but they remind us that every leader has to be taking their people towards something.

Although it is vital to set the example of how to work effectively in a changing world – and I have so far paid a lot of attention to that aspect of leadership – it is also vital to give the working practice some purpose and direction.

## looking to the future

Traditional working practice has tended to be oriented to the past rather than the future. People have been encouraged to maintain the customs and traditions of the organization, and there has been a hope that this would be enough to keep the organization going. In the last few decades, we have seen many examples of large businesses failing because they continued to work on the premise that doing what they have always done would pay off. It is also a common theme at an individual level. People will resist a new idea or a new approach by defending their present practice and saying, 'We have always done it like this – it's tried and tested.'

In a rapidly changing world, it is those who have a future orientation who will succeed. This applies at organizational level – it is the businesses that are actively looking for new opportunities and new ways of working that thrive – and it also applies at the individual level.

Whether you are Richard Branson, constantly exploring new markets and new approaches, or an estates department manager, noticing that technology is reducing the need for high street outlets and enabling new approaches to working practice in the department, you need to be someone who can look forward and plan for an unpredictable future. What is more, you need to be able to take others with you in that future orientation, and convince them that there is something worthwhile to strive for.

There are two areas to explore in setting a direction:

■ The long-term and short-term vision of what we will achieve.
■ The working practice that will enable us to achieve it.

# the long-term vision

We still have a tendency to work towards short-term goals and to make them very concrete – a sales target for the month, or the finishing of a project in three months. These are important but they are not enough.

A long-term vision puts these short-term goals into context, and enables people to see how their achievement is more than an end in itself. The long-term vision also provides more than just a context for short-term goals. It provides a context for improving practice, so that all goals become easier to achieve, because everyone is working in the most effective way.

> The new director for IT in a major manufacturing company knew what he wanted to achieve. He wanted his team's work to become central to the business, providing the strategic support for the business to be successful.
>
> When he joined the company, his team were generally considered to be 'techies' who lived in an ivory tower, with little relevance to the mainstream business.
>
> His vision required more than meeting targets. It required changes in attitude, changes in behaviour, and careful strategic planning.

## how do you set a long-term vision?

Long-term visions are about ideals. You need to aim high and imagine how you would like work to be. Setting a vision is about possibility and potential rather than necessity and realism.

*What is your vision for your area of work? Think of how, ideally, you would like it to be in two to five years' time. At this stage, do not consider all the things you think would stop you from achieving this. As you develop your vision, you will notice that you begin to imagine not just what will be achieved, but also how people will be behaving as they achieve it. (By the way, your vision may be something you picture, or you may just use words to describe it. Either way works equally well.)*

Once you have begun to imagine for yourself what you would like to achieve, and how, you have already set in motion the possibility. The next stage is to involve your team in the vision.

## sharing your vision

If your team don't buy in to your vision, you will be ploughing a lone furrow. You need to involve them as early in the process as possible and gain their commitment to the same ideal.

First you have to describe your vision to them. It is important to think carefully about how you would word it, because you want them to find the ideas attractive.

*Think about what will make your vision attractive to your team. Is it going to make life easier for them, enhance their reputation, build on their strengths, give them skills that make them more employable? (If there is nothing you can think of that will make it attractive to them, maybe you need to think again!)*

Remember, as you present your vision, that your passion and enthusiasm for it will have a powerful impact. It is not enough to think through your wording; you must also have feeling involved. You want your team to buy in, not just on an intellectual level, but also at a feeling level.

Then I would suggest that you build on that vision with them, just as you did when you imagined it for yourself. This is a very powerful mechanism and is what gains their buy-in. You ask them to imagine that you have achieved the ideal that you are setting out, and then to imagine what the working practice will be like in this ideal vision. When I do this, I always ask teams to work in smaller groups and come up with a metaphor for the working practice. Examples would be:

- We are like the Star Trek team, running the ship perfectly and dealing effectively with any problems.
- We are like a world-class sports team, each playing their role to achieve the end result.
- We are like an orchestra, with different people taking the lead at different times and producing a beautiful symphony.

Each group first makes a selection from the suggestions they have for a metaphor, then lists what the metaphor implies about how they would work. This is fun to do but also produces fascinating results, as you will find out when you try it. Even though the groups may have chosen different metaphors, the definition of the ideal working practice they produce through the implications they list are virtually identical. Typical statements would be:

- We work co-operatively.
- Everyone has something to contribute.
- We all help out if there are any problems.
- We have fun yet work hard.
- We know what we're doing and why we're doing it, so we just get on with it.
- We accept that sometimes there are mistakes and all work to learn from them and put them right.
- We constantly check that we're still on course.
- We learn from each other.
- We respect each other's different qualities and skills.
- We keep each other's spirits up and encourage each other.
- We remember to have a life outside work.

If you ask your team to do this activity, they will discover that your vision is attractive for themselves, so there will be automatic buy-in – and they will also have begun to define the working practice that will help you to achieve it!

*Are you prepared to take the risk of involving your team in defining the full picture of how your vision will work? It may seem risky, but I assure you that it isn't. The results I have seen suggest that the ideal working practice for achieving extraordinary results is defined in virtually the same way in any organization in any country.*

## confirming the vision as a possibility

Some of your team will undoubtedly be wanting to remind you of 'the real world', if you're not doing that already yourself!

We all have many more examples of 'failure' than we do of success, and we tend to immediately jump in and say why something won't work. This strategy may seem wise, but it is often the reason why achievements are limited.

If we consciously decide to look for examples that support the possibility of achieving both the what and the how of the vision, we build up our belief that it is achievable.

*Think for a moment about your vision. Where have people achieved similar visions? This can be in business or in their personal life. Think of as many examples as you can, big and small. Now think about the elements of the ideal working practice. Where have you personally put some of those elements into practice and where have you seen others working like this?*

Once you begin to think of examples, many will begin to come to you. It may be at the level of Richard Branson or Albert Einstein; it may be your local shop or community group; it may be your old manager. And you will realize that you have often practised the elements of ideal working practice, even if not in the workplace!

*You could do the activity with your whole team, and build up a portfolio of success stories.*

Once we realize that there is plenty of evidence that it is possible to achieve visions like ours, we become more committed to making it happen.

## the Walt Disney model

What I have described so far fits well with the strategy used by Walt Disney to create successful films, as described by Robert Dilts in *Tools for Dreamers*.
Disney split the process into three parts:

1. The dreamer.
2. The realist.
3. The critic.

The dreamer stage is where you just have ideas, as if anything were possible. This corresponds to your vision in the first place, and then the process of getting 'buy-in' from your team to the overall vision.

The realist stage is where you make plans to make it happen. Again, possible obstacles are not dealt with at this stage – we save them for the critic stage. The realist acts as if this 'dream' or vision can be made to happen, and works out how.

## turning the vision into reality – the realist stage

Once you have defined the ideal in terms of what you want to achieve and the working practice that will go along with it, you can begin to plan the steps towards it. There are various ways of describing this process – it may be called objective-setting or goal-setting.

If you involve the whole team in this planning it will be more constructive and you won't then have to gain their agreement afterwards. And if you have successfully communicated and shared your vision, you will all be working towards the same end.

A metaphor for this process would be the creation of a garden. If you move to a house that has only bare earth around it, you start by imagining the garden you would like to create. Then you assess the state of the soil and decide whether you need to fertilize it, shape it differently, what you will begin to plant, etc. Now you have strategies to take you from the current reality towards your vision.

*I would suggest you have two sub-groups, one looking at the plan for the 'what' of the vision, the other looking at the working practice required – the 'how'.*

## mind-mapping

To make this planning easier, you could use mind-mapping in the first place. (If you don't already know the technique, read Tony Buzan's work on this.) With this technique, all the possible steps required are recorded on one sheet of paper, in any order that they occur to people, with sub-groupings if appropriate.

This technique can be used with both parts of the planning, and obviously some areas may require more detailed analysis at a later stage. This just gives you main headings. See Figure 12.1 for an example.

From the mind-map you can then jointly agree the order of the developments. With all the main ideas in front of you on one sheet of paper, you can easily highlight the priorities and the first steps you will need to make. At this stage you can produce an action plan which clearly indicates the stages of development towards your vision. It may look something like this.

|  | **Initial phase** | **By whom** | **By when** |
|---|---|---|---|
|  | **Action** |  |  |
| *The vision* | Assessing our current position | Whole team | At next team meeting |
| *The vision* | Asking for feedback from others – Jack to devise questions and distribute to team, then each to ask their main contacts | Jack and whole team | Before next team meeting |

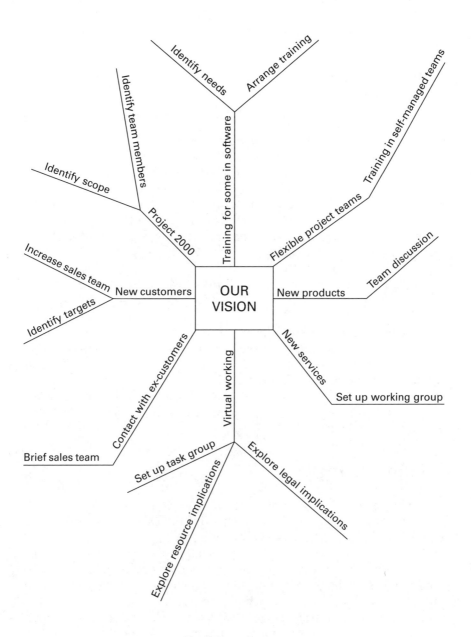

**Figure 12.1**

| | | | |
|---|---|---|---|
| *Working practice* | Devising ground rules for how we work as a team – to be presented, discussed and agreed by the team | Sarah, Jim and Jane | Next team meeting |
| *Working practice* | Informing our own teams about what we're looking at | Whole team | Next team talk session |

Notice that this starts pinning down responsibilities and timing, and that the statements give clear objectives, so that you can monitor your progress against the plan. It can take quite a while to go through this stage, and some of the plan may be more detailed than other parts. What this gives you is a basis to assess your progress against and develop details further. It is important that your plan includes both development towards the vision and development of your working practice, running at the same time. Your vision's achievement requires both parts if it is to succeed.

*Try out this stage of the process with your team. Remember that the underlying assumption is that it is possible to achieve the vision.*

This is a basic formula for producing a business plan, extended to include 'how' as well as 'what' you will achieve. It can take into account the strategic objectives of your business, and go further to include a larger vision. You can use it at various levels of detail, depending on what suits you. For example, you may decide to break down the action steps into smaller chunks, using the same method, to produce monthly plans rather than annual plans or longer.

## using the critic

Once you have your plans drafted, it's time to allow the 'critic' to check it over. Disney's use of the critic is constructive rather than destructive, and is a very useful tool when used in the right place.

The critic checks the plan to identify anything that might stop it working. He or she does this by asking questions rather than simply stating obstacles – on seeing something that looks like a problem, he or she composes a question. An example from the action plan might be: 'How will we ensure that we all give the same message to our teams?' This may prompt a group discussion to identify key points you all agree to pass on.

Other sample questions might be:

- How do we get others to co-operate with us?
- How will we persuade x to let us do this?
- How will we fund this activity?
- How will we develop the skills to do this?
- What will we do if the budget is cut?
- What will we do if we don't get agreement?
- What links this action to our mission?
- What makes this an important part of our strategy?

Notice that all the questions start with 'what' or 'how'. They automatically prompt your brain to think through an action you can take, rather than just justify the particular item. It is very important that you formulate all the questions this way.

*It can be very useful to take a sub-group of your team to do this 'critic' activity. I would choose those who most often tend to take this role anyway, as it shows them how to criticize constructively. You can either ask them just to raise the questions to take back to the whole team, or ask them to find answers to their own questions, in 'realist' mode.*

You can now revise your plan to include the extras to deal with the points they have raised.

## identifying what you already have

You now have a plan to turn your vision into reality. It can look daunting, especially if you have dared to go for a dream rather than limited it from the start. It is important, therefore, to recognize that you are never starting from scratch.

We always have some stock of experience, skills, attitudes, behaviours and previous actions that will help us to achieve our vision. This applies to both parts of the vision: what we want to achieve and the working practice we want to have. If you can identify this stock, the vision will immediately feel more achievable.

*Ask your team to look at the plan and the vision and identify what they already have, between them, that will help to achieve this. Use the terms I gave in the previous paragraph – experience, skills, attitudes, behaviours, previous actions.*

This is a very positive activity, because it identifies the strengths and contributions of the team and of members within it. It doesn't matter if the whole team can't claim a particular attitude, behaviour, or skill, so long as it is there in the team. People feel good when their potential contributions are identified, particularly when they are in categories that are not traditionally recognized as contributions, such as being optimistic, or helping to keep everyone's mood buoyant. And by identifying who has the attribute, you are increasing the likelihood of them using it.

Once you have made this list, the achievement of your vision won't look so daunting. You already have the foundation in place and can now build on it.

# identifying priorities

It is important to consider how you can turn your plan into action in a way that is motivating and realistic. You can use your logical mind to decide on priorities, and you will identify some. But you can also use your creative mind to help you to identify the essential elements that your rational mind may miss out. For this, I recommend the use of 'wisdom with hindsight beforehand'.

## *wisdom with hindsight beforehand*
We all have a remarkable ability to have wisdom with hindsight: 'If only I had paid attention when she told me she was fed up, I might have been able to avoid her resigning,' or 'If only I had realized that my attitude towards that team was affecting how they behaved.'

It seems to me that we could use this ability more constructively by applying it before the event instead of afterwards. We are, after all, also very good at 'predicting' the future. We imagine how some event will go beforehand and are often very accurate – this is sometimes called 'a self-fulfilling prophecy'!

I have already suggested that you imagine the vision being achieved, to identify what needs to be done and what working practice you need to achieve it. The more often you and your team do this, the more you set up the circuitry in your creative mind to enable you to achieve it. So using wisdom with hindsight beforehand will give you another chance to do this.

It requires that you imagine that you have achieved your vision. Then, looking back to the present, you ask yourselves, 'What made the most difference to us achieving the vision?' 'What were the most important steps we took?' and allow your answers to come into your mind. It's a bit like being the director of a film: you are looking for the leverage points that make the project a success. In my experience, the answers that come up are more likely to be about behaviours and attitudes and ways of reinforcing those, than about particular actions. These are the underlying things that make the difference, which don't 'show' in the same way as the actions do, but which enable the actions to be effective.

*Apply wisdom with hindsight beforehand with your team. Remember that this is an activity that uses the creative side of your brain. You may like to physically move everyone to another part of the room and call that space the 'achieved vision' space. This can help to switch on our creativity. Then they can look back literally to where they were to represent the starting point. Ask everyone to feel as if they have achieved the vision: be delighted, satisfied, enjoying it. Then ask the questions and record the answers.*

*Note that some answers may seem 'off the wall' to your logical mind. Accept them anyway. They may be the most useful – remember, geniuses are people who don't stick to the logical!*

> I was preparing for a presentation that was very important for me. I had thought through what I wanted to get across to the audience and how I wanted to be. I decided to apply wisdom with hindsight before-hand to the situation. When I asked myself 'What made the most difference to achieving what I wanted?', the answer that came up was that I set aside an hour before I left to give the presentation and had a long soak in a bath. It didn't seem very logical, but I did it anyway.
>
> And it was marvellous! I left behind all the 'stuff' from the morning, I relaxed, and I felt refreshed and comfortable. It put me into a state that made it easy to achieve what I wanted to achieve. My creative mind gave me something I wouldn't normally have thought of and it worked.

When you combine your logically thought-out priorities with those that come from your creative mind, you will know, as a team, what you can do to make the most difference to achieving your wisdom.

## the first steps

After you have done this work, you will have a comprehensive plan for achieving your vision. Now you need to make a start. At this point I recommend you remember how we are motivated. We all like to have some 'quick wins'. You obviously need to start working on your priorities, but you also need to feel that you're making real progress. What have you got in your plan that could be achieved relatively easily? One or two things

**131**

that could be crossed off the list quickly should be in your first action plan. This will help to keep the momentum going.

If all your actions are ones which will take a lot of work, break a couple of them down into smaller steps so that you can identify progress as you go, rather than feeling like you're getting nowhere and so becoming disheartened.

*Identify first steps with your team, with people taking responsibility for making them happen, even if they won't personally do the whole thing. Make sure that they are easily achievable.*

## time to plan for the vision

You cannot do this work on creating a vision of the future as a ten-minute slot in your weekly meeting. It requires more time and space. I would recommend that you take two days out of your normal work, either as two days together or as two separate days. It is also worthwhile locating it somewhere outside work so that you are not distracted by the normal demands on your attention. A pleasant environment with a nice lunch can make a lot of difference to the way in which people approach this activity.

You may think you cannot afford this time. I would suggest to you that you cannot afford not to do this. In two days, you and your team can produce a plan to make your business even more effective in the future, which will be your blueprint for success. You waste far more time than that coping with the problems that arise from only working on a short-term basis. We need to be prepared to invest in quality work, rather than just look at time spent like this as a cost.

# maintaining the movement towards the vision

After a planning session like this, people are usually enthused, and rush off to complete the first stages of the plan. Then they get caught up again in the immediate crisis of everyday work and lose sight of the longer term, if there is not a defined prompt to keep the momentum going.

This is particularly true of the working practice side of the vision. We are so used to working hard rather than smart, and to neglecting relationships and process in favour of short-term results, that it is vital to keep the momentum going on achieving the 'how' as well as the 'what'.

In organizations of the future, the working practice will be even more important than it is now. How people work together, how they tackle problems, how they use their creativity, how they deal with customers, and how they enjoy their work will be the leverage points which will distinguish the successful from the unsuccessful.

Ricardo Semler is CEO of a successful company in Brazil, whose working practice is radically different from the traditional boss. His company is visited by people from all over the world, because it is a prime example of a 21st century organization. Ricardo says, 'My main job is to ensure that people really want to come to work on Monday mornings.' His view is that if the working practice is right, people will be motivated and success will follow. And he has over a decade of evidence that it's true.

# how do you maintain the momentum?

You need to assign meetings to review progress and achievements and to set the next steps on a regular basis. These meetings need to be separate from your normal team meetings, even if the separation is to assign two extra hours once a month to the normal meeting and to have the review meeting first, then take a break and run your normal meeting. I have suggested that the review meeting comes first for three reasons:

1.  It deserves priority – it is very important.
2.  It will help set a positive tone for your normal meeting.
3.  You cannot then allow the normal meeting to over-run and reduce the time allocated for the review.

## format for the meetings
These meetings should have a set agenda:

1.  *Celebrate successes* – everyone to identify achievements and progress against your plan.
2.  *Identify and deal with sticking points* – where things are not going to plan, avoid the 'blame' syndrome. Just identify the sticking points, whether individual or for the team as a whole, and use your combined brain power to plan to deal with them.
3.  *Celebrate learning* – look at mistakes you have made and what you have learned from them.

4. *Review the overall plan* – put together your short-term action plan to deal with sticking points, incorporate learning, and continue your progress towards the overall plan.

It is very important to have item 1 on the agenda. People need to be constantly reminded that they are making progress if they are to stay motivated. This is particularly true for those whose tasks may take a longer period to complete, or those who only contribute partly to any achievements. Similarly, item 3 makes sure that you don't get into the blame culture syndrome of finding fault. Mistakes or things going wrong are part of the progress, not failures.

> I was talking to Pat, administrative assistant to the director, about how they were doing with their plan. She said that she had thought that she didn't have an important part to play, until they started doing the review meetings. Then she realized that she could and did help considerably, not only by doing the back-up administration efficiently, but also by helping to maintain the working practice side of the plan. She was a key player in this, reminding people gently of the ground rules they had all agreed, and setting an example for putting them into practice. Having this acknowledged every month by the rest of the team really motivated her, and she was now looking at ways she could contribute even more.

## application to self-development

This approach to setting a direction can equally well be applied at an individual level. All the steps are the same, and are best done with a mentor of some sort. This gives us the extra support and reinforcement that helps us to keep going with it.

## conclusion

As a 21st century manager, you need to be able to give your team direction. Even if the overall business objectives change, you can easily revise this form of business plan to meet the new objectives. If you have paid attention to how you work as a team, as well as what you work on, you will find it even easier to deal with change, because you are already working as a flexible, co-operative team.

Your personal willingness to share your vision and have others contribute to how it may be achieved will set an example of how to approach things co-operatively and 'give away' control, without losing power or leadership.

# influencing

By now you will realize that the excellent manager of the future will not be a traditional command and control manager. That style is not one that brings out the best in people, and that will be your job, above all. So you will need to develop further your skills of influencing, to achieve what you want to achieve with the willing co-operation of your staff.

Although we have already covered some of the aspects of excellent influencing in exploring communicating and self-management, it's worthwhile looking specifically at this skill as it is so central to your role.

## what influencing means

The etymology of the word 'influence' is 'to flow into'. It is important to remember this. It reminds us that excellent influencing is not intrusive, but flows naturally into the person's existing way of being.

I like to use the metaphor of a stream joining a river. It matches the flow, the direction and the current of the river, and joins the river effortlessly. Yet it may well help to alter the course of the river from that point on.

When people try to change the course of a river, they will build a dam to block its natural course. In some instances, the river will simply revert to its natural course after it has got past the dam. If the dam is powerful enough to stop the river doing this, there is usually significant ecological damage both up- and downstream of the dam.

### poor influencing

All too often, so-called influencing is more like the artificial version than the natural one. Either people just pay lip service to a change, but carry on exactly as they were, or, if they are forced to make the change, it causes them and their environment significant damage.

If you're not convinced, stop and think about it for a moment. How many organizations have some form of valuing diversity or equal opportunities policy, yet still give most value to conformity to the norm? How many organizations have 'empowered' their employees, yet still have managers who tell people that they can't show initiative because they are not empowered in that way? It is very common for organizations to implement a policy to which only lip service is paid, and the more often this happens, the more likely people are to revert to their previous behaviour, because they assume that it is only a 'flavour of the month' and won't be followed through. They think that if they keep their heads down, the storm will blow over and things will get back to normal.

*Have you ever felt like this about a change in your organization?*

And what if an organizational change is forced on people, if there is no way round it? This also has been very common. For example, re-structuring, de-layering, or whatever else it may be called, has been seen as the way forward in many organizations. It is a fast way of achieving cost cutting, and has frequently been applied in a non-negotiable and poorly thought through way.

The principle of de-layering is a good one, but it involves a far more thorough process than has happened in most organizations that have applied it. If accompanied by a careful check to see which posts could genuinely be removed from the structure, plus preparation of employees for the change through genuine empowerment and retraining, as well as guidance on how to work smarter and a revised management style, it can be effective. This, however, has not been the norm. And the results are there for all to see.

There is the obvious damage to most of those who are made redundant, who are put under enormous stress, losing self-esteem and anxious about whether they will find alternative work. And then there is what is called the 'survivor's syndrome'. Those who are still in a job also suffer high levels of stress and anxiety. They are not sure of their new responsibilities, they feel that they have to work even harder in case there are further staff cuts, and they feel guilty that they survived when colleagues didn't. This causes problems, not just for them individually, but also for the organization, because their morale and their sense of loyalty are lowered. I'm sure that you can think of both organizational and individual examples of poor influencing, where it was either ineffective or damaging.

## excellent influencing

When we compare the above description with excellent influencing, we can really recognize the difference. An excellent influencer recognizes and acknowledges your world view, and works with it – a stream joining the flow of the river. Consequently, we feel comfortable with the resulting change and can own it as fitting for us.

When I first went to college, I had a very narrow view of learning, believing that it was linked to being taught subjects, as I had experienced in school. One of my tutors talked with me over the first term about learning. He was enthusiastic about the subject, but also respectful of my view, gradually encouraging me to notice that I was learning how, not just what. He would ask questions like: 'What did you learn about that theory?' After I had answered that, he would ask: 'How did you learn that?' I began to realize that learning is a never-ending process, if you decide to open yourself to it, and that there are lots of sources of learning, not just books and teachers.

His approach made it make sense to me, and broadened my view without destroying what I already had.

*Think of examples of your own where someone has been a positive influence for you. It may be long term where you had contact with them for a good while, such as parents, teachers, friends, work colleagues, or it may have been a one-off influence, such as an excellent conference speaker, a tape you heard, or someone you met on a train. Just think about what it was that enabled you to be influenced by them.*

## the elements of excellent influencing

An excellent influencer has a certain air about them. They give off a sense of integrity – you feel that they are not out to cause you any harm – and they are clearly committed wholeheartedly to what they are putting forward. This shows in their enthusiasm, but it is not the enthusiasm of a fanatic who wants to 'convert' you to their way of thinking - they are not forcing their point of view down your throat. Instead, they present it in a way that makes sense in your world, and you feel as if they understand and appreciate your point of view. It is irresistible to go along with them, yet it feels as if it is your choice to do so.

## so how do we get to be excellent influencers?

First of all, you need to recognize that sometimes you are an excellent influencer! All of us have influenced others well in some situations, often without realizing it. For instance, you may have influenced your child to join the scouts or guides, or you may have influenced a colleague to react less negatively.

> *Think now of a time when you have influenced someone excellently. As you remember that time, notice how you are when you influence effectively: your body posture, your tone of voice, the way you are thinking about the person and the situation.*

# the way you are when you influence well

You will notice that I asked you to think about how you are when you influence effectively – physically and mentally. An excellent influencer first of all sets themselves up so that they come across in such a way as to make the other person feel that they are willing to be influenced. You cannot put this on as a façade, because people can instinctively spot the 'front', so you need to be genuine in your integrity and enthusiasm.

## what you want to influence

First you need to consider exactly what influence you wish to have on this person. Think about it carefully. Will it have a useful long-term effect for them? If not, you may need to re-think.

If you re-read the first part of Chapter 10, you will be reminded about setting your intentions and outcomes in a way that matches with the other person's world. You will then come across as having a genuine intention to make a positive difference to them.

## your beliefs about the outcomes of the influence

If you are not convinced that the outcome is a worthwhile one, then you will certainly never convince someone else.

> When I was a teacher, I was told that I must make the pupils line up quietly outside the class before letting them in and beginning the lesson. I couldn't really see the point of this, but I dutifully tried to enforce the rule, to no avail. The pupils played up and messed about, and I lost a lot of time out of my lessons just trying to make this work.
>
> So I had to re-think. There were two outcomes I *did* feel strongly about:

- That they and I avoided trouble from the headmaster.
- That we had the full lesson time.

When I suggested that we obey the rule, in order to have these two outcomes, with the promise that I would make the lessons interesting to them, the pupils agreed, so the rule was obeyed, not for its original purpose of discipline, but for outcomes that appealed to both me and the pupils.

*Think about an influence you would like to have in the workplace. Consider the outcomes you want and what will make them convincing, for you and for the person(s) to be influenced.*

## how you are when you influence

Once you have clarified your thoughts about influencing, they will automatically affect the way you approach the person, in terms of physical posture and voice tone. It is important, though, just to check that you are not evangelical because of your conviction about the rightness of the influence.

Remind yourself of how you were physically, and what you sounded like when you influenced excellently. This will help you to tone down any over-reaction. Another way in which we can ensure that we come across as we intend is to complete the process of preparing to influence.

## joining the river

We cannot influence others effectively unless we recognize what their world is like. You cannot take it for granted that you already know. To join their river effectively, you first need to step into the river and discover what it is like to be in their world. This doesn't mean that you have to literally experience what they experience. It does mean that you have to find out about their world in a non-judgemental way.

When I was a youth worker, I worked with a gang of so-called delinquents. I wanted to find out what it was like to be them, so I sat with them and asked lots of questions. They liked having someone who was genuinely interested in how they saw the world and how they operated in it, and I discovered information that enabled me to work with them far more effectively, because I knew what motivated them and what rules they lived by.

# asking the right questions

If you want to find out about someone's world, you have to make sure that you ask the right questions. The first rule is: don't ask why. 'Why' is our most common question, and it has unfortunate implications:

■ that what they have said makes no sense to us;
■ that what they have said is wrong.

Think about this for a moment and you will see what I mean. If you agree with the way someone has performed a task, you are unlikely to ask them, 'Why did you do it that way?' This question occurs when you don't understand their reason for approaching the task in the way they did, or when you think they performed it in the wrong way.

The effect of the question, 'Why did you do it that way?' is that the person feels criticized and immediately becomes defensive, or else they feel that you have not appreciated their way of doing things and do not understand them. This means that they feel judged and give you far less useful information.

Instead, you can ask, 'What prompted you to take that approach?' or, 'How did you decide on the approach you took to the task?' With either of these questions, you will find out how they think things through, and what matters to them in performing a task.

So, instead of 'why' questions, ask 'how' or 'what'. A question that begins with these two will usually elicit useful information.

## leading questions

Beware of leading questions. These are questions like: 'Have you thought of . . .' or 'Don't you think that . . .?' They are not really genuine questions at all. They don't find out about the other person's world – they tell them about your world and ask them if they agree with it or not.

## useful questions for finding out about their world

If you want to find out about someone's world, the following are some useful questions to ask:

■ What do you enjoy about . . .?
■ What matters to you about . . .?
■ How do you approach . . .?
■ What makes you feel good?
■ How do you motivate yourself to . . .?
■ What made you choose . . .?
■ How do you feel about . . .?
■ What's important to you in . . .?

You can apply these questions to almost anything, from the universal 'your life' to the specific – a particular situation or task.

## using the questions in context

Obviously, if you just walked up to someone whom you want to influence and started asking them these questions about their life or their work, it would feel like an inquisition. You need to use these questions in the context of the person talking about themselves. Most of the time, I would start to find out about someone's world by asking them if they would tell me something about their work. As they start to talk, I ask the questions where they are relevant. In my experience, people enjoy being the centre of attention in this way and can give you a lot of information about their world in quite a brief space of time.

It is important to approach this with a spirit of curiosity. Children are very good at it, and you need that same attitude of genuine interest and non-judgement. Remind yourself of how to pay genuine attention, as described in Chapter 11.

> *Practise finding out about others' worlds. Find more out about a relative, a friend, a colleague, a member of your staff. Do it over coffee, or a lunch-break, in an informal way, so that you get comfortable with asking the questions and with being genuinely curious rather than judgemental.*

# 'I already know about their river'

A question arises for me whenever anyone says they already know about someone else's world: 'Are you able to influence them effectively, whenever it is appropriate?' We often find out some things about how people tick and then assume the rest.

This is a particular danger if we think they are 'like us'. If they value some of the same things that we do, if we share interests, we assume that we also share other things, like what motivates us, or how we approach things. Just check that they really are 'like you' before you make that assumption.

# 'I have to influence a whole group – how can I find out about all of them?'

Sometimes it's not possible to find out in detail about everyone you are wanting to influence, for example at a large presentation. In this case you need to plan to influence by using what information you do have about them, plus using a variety of possible reasons why they may want to be influenced. Then watch and listen carefully, in the influencing process. People will give you feedback, verbal and non-verbal, which tells you how successful you are being. If you have prepared a range of approaches to your subject, you can change tack if one isn't working and try something different.

## using the information you have gathered

You will notice that all the work so far is about preparing to be an excellent influencer. Although we do sometimes influence well without any conscious preparation, most of us are far more effective if we prepare ourselves and find out about the river we are intending to join.

Now we can plan to influence. From the information you have gathered, ask yourself the following questions:

- What exactly do I want as an outcome (short term and long term)?
- How do I make that outcome fit with their world? (What matters to them, relates to their world.)
- What type of approach do I need to use to make this comfortable for them (formal or informal)?
- Where and when would be the best for them to accept the influence (appropriate time and place)?
- How will I be when I am influencing them (physical positioning, voice tone, conviction)?

Your answers to these questions will give you the basic action plan for influencing.

A new MD had been appointed to a large IT company. He wanted to show his staff that he was approachable and that he needed their co-operation to make some significant changes in the culture of the company. He knew that people feared that his appointment would mean more restructuring and job losses, because they had heard that he was appointed to make changes.

He noticed that there were two types of meetings: the very formal ones, with senior staff present, and the more relaxed ones for the smaller teams. He knew that he would be expected to introduce himself and his expectations at a larger formal meeting, but he decided to ask the teams if he could be an item on the agenda for their next meeting.

He made it clear that he wanted 20 minutes and that he would like to be positioned on the agenda before a coffee-break if possible.

The first team he visited had arranged for an OHP and a lectern to be in the room, assuming that he would give a formal presentation. Instead, he sat down at the table with them and talked about himself, his history and his plans in an informal way. He made it clear that he wanted cultural and structural change, but no job losses. He finished on time and stayed for the coffee-break, asking people what they thought of his plans.

Although he only got polite answers, he had had the effect he wanted. When he went to the next team meeting, the grapevine had already passed the message on: there was no lectern or OHP, just an extra chair at the table. And when he asked people what they thought of his plans, he began to get some constructive responses.

*What influence do you want to have on your team in the near future? Go through the full process of preparation I have described, and plan to have that influence.*

## remembering the longer term

The example I have given above is typical of much of our influencing. We want to effect changes in attitude or behaviour that are not going to occur as a result of one-off influencing. This MD's behaviour and approach in his first encounter with his staff opened the door for him to have an influence. He then had to maintain, reinforce and build on that, to really have an effect.

I was talking to one of his managers some six months after his appointment. 'He really meant what he said!' she told me. When I asked her what made her say that, she said that he had published clear details of his plans in a very readable form, he had made time in his diary for people to come and give him their feedback on his plans, and had listened, discussed and made amendments from the feedback. He also got to know people's names and was now a welcome visitor to team meetings.

*What do you need to be aware of for longer-term influencing? What effect do you want to have on your staff? Think about two everyday behaviours that you have or could develop to maintain your effective influencing.*

## conclusion

You are already influencing others all the time. The question is whether it is the influence which joins their river, feels natural, and helps them to develop, or if it is a form of dam which may force a change, but doesn't have a useful long-term effect.

It doesn't take a lot of time to prepare to be an effective influencer. It does have big pay-offs, for those you influence and for you. After all, life is a lot easier when people do what you want without being forced to. As a 21st century manager you want to affect in a positive way the performance of your staff, without becoming a dam. Being an excellent influencer will enable you to inspire rather than force your staff to be at their best and to use their skills well.

## endpiece

## and if you fail to communicate effectively

It is not easy to be consistent in this area. There are times when we react rather than respond, and we fail to maintain good rapport. And there are times when we don't get our message across in the way we wanted to.

I suggest you try some of the following when your communication isn't working:

- *Walk away:* if your state isn't right, and you are just getting more frustrated, go away and recover yourself. Apologize to the person concerned and take responsibility for the effect you have had.
- *Have another go:* it is very effective to say that you have not put your message across how you wanted to, and that you would like to have another go. Try a different tack, or a different method of getting your message across.
- *Review what happened:* play it through again in your head, noticing what threw you off balance, and then play through how you will tackle it differently next time.
- *Remember your good moments:* it is so important not to get caught up in your failures. Remind yourself of several of your good communication situations and get that circuitry running in your head, ready for the next time.

No one is perfect in their communication, and the best way to improve your skills in this area is to learn from your mistakes and from your own good practice.

## Part IV

# Managing Others

If you have applied the principles in the other sections of this book, then managing others will already have become a lot easier.

Excellent managers begin by being in control of themselves, and by developing their communication skills. As we approach the 21st century, these skills will become ever more important, because the leverage point in competition for business will be the way people approach their work, and that will depend largely on how they are managed.

In this section, we will look at some particular aspects of managing others which have not yet been specifically covered. They highlight some of the most important ways in which we need to adapt our management style to ensure that our employees give of their best in the workplace. They also relate to the situations where there is the greatest danger of falling back into traditional management habits, doing what has been done to us in the past, even though we know that it is not the most effective way of achieving the result we want.

It is easy as a manager to get so caught up in tasks, targets and crises that we do not allow ourselves the time to work at the people processes which make a significant difference to the way people contribute at work. It is also sometimes far more satisfying to have done a task than to continue the long-term process of managing people, which doesn't give you the same hard evidence of achievement.

Yet these people processes will enhance the achievements of your business far more than you alone can. And your role will be that of facilitator, not obvious in terms of doing things, but vital in ensuring that things are done.

# motivating **others**

This is probably the most crucial part of your job. Unless your staff are motivated, you will not have a thriving business. You may continue to work, if you are lucky, but you will not have a business that is going to survive.

Motivation means putting into motion or moving. Every organization will need to be moving or dynamic in the 21st century, and the dynamism of the business will depend on the dynamism of the people involved.

I am not talking here about getting the job done. I am talking about the enthusiasm which produces more than that. We all know the difference between doing something because we have to – it's a duty or obligation – and doing something because we want to – we're motivated to do it well.

> As a simple example, observe your neighbours' gardens. There will be some that are clearly dutiful – reasonably neat, but uninspired. Then there are those that are tended with enthusiasm, not always the tidiest, but with interesting, different layouts and plants. They catch our attention because they have a different spirit to them.

It is similar with organizations. You can feel the difference in spirit as soon as you enter the building.

> I was invited to meet the manufacturing directors of a major car company. As I drove into the business unit where the meeting was taking place, my heart sank. The site was grey, cluttered and noisy. It didn't improve when I went inside for the meeting. The general sense was of doing what had to be done. One of the directors obviously noticed my reaction. 'Do come and visit us on our site,' he said. 'It's very different from this.'
>
> I agreed to go, and at first sight it didn't look particularly different. But the security guards greeted me differently, there was a parking space

for me, the receptionist was expecting me and smiled, and I began to sense that there was indeed a different spirit to this site. I asked the director who had invited me what he thought made the difference. 'We all love our product, and we're like a family here – we care about each other, all muck in when there's a problem, all delight in our success.'

He didn't mention anything to do with motivation, but it was clearly there.

## where does motivation come from?

The title of this chapter is misleading in a sense, because we cannot motivate others. Motivation is always self-motivation. It is a decision on the part of the individual to move into action. This decision is made when there are enough motivating factors involved to make it worth our while. Notice that for most of us, there is more than one motivating factor needed.

It is one of the myths of working life that if you give people lots of money for what they do, they will be motivated. This may work on a short-term basis, but it is certainly not enough to maintain motivation.

In a study I conducted into good practice in people management, I asked the managers concerned what they found motivated people to perform well. They all came up with answers that fitted under four headings:

1. Respect.
2. Recognition.
3. Responsibility.
4. Recreation.

They were clear that one of these on its own was not enough. All these areas were required.

As a manager, you cannot make people be motivated, but you can set up an environment where the motivating factors are available so that they are more likely to decide to be motivated.

## why do we want motivation?

As managers, we need to be convinced that we want motivated staff before we will work at setting the right environment for motivation. After all, there has been some history of preferring those who just get on with their job quietly in a way that meets minimum requirements.

I remember taking a holiday job as a 'clerical assistant' in a clinic. My job was to file the patients' folders from the previous day and get out those needed for the next day. Then I had to make sure all the folders were filed correctly. After four days, I had gone through the whole filing system and made sure everything was in order. The daily part of the job took me less than an hour. I suggested to my supervisor that I could do something else. She told me that I should stop trying to show others up and just look busy! I soon became very bored.

We still hear comments like, 'He's just been on a training course, but he'll soon get over it,' or 'She's new here, and wants to make an impression, but we'll sort her out.'

## motivated people make changes happen

In the 21st century we will need everyone at work to have the enthusiasm and motivation of the new starter or the freshly trained. Organizations will be dealing with constant change, in technology and in the business environment. We want people who want to learn and change and develop, people who will contribute change and innovation themselves. Even if their job stays the same, we want them to be constantly looking for ways of improving the process. This only happens when people are motivated.

*Think of times when you have been really motivated. Notice how differently you approach what you are doing.*

## making management easy

The second reason for wanting motivated people is very selfish – it makes management of them easy. In order to achieve your visions you will want people who are actively involved, who want to develop their working practice, and who will help you to set up that different spirit in your organization.

If you don't have to drag them into the 21st century, you can devote your energies to setting the direction so they have a framework to work in, and to providing the motivational environment. As Semler said, your job becomes ensuring that they continue to want to come to work. And this is a far more enjoyable task than trying to make people do things that they don't particularly want to.

# the motivating factors

How do we set up the motivational environment? We begin by ensuring that the motivational factors that we can influence are in place. These factors relate closely to what people usually come up with when they do the metaphor exercise I described in Chapter 12. Let us look at each of the main areas of motivation in turn.

## respect

Respect consists of several elements, and is an essential part of working practice if people are to be motivated. Respect makes people feel that they matter and are important to the organization.

First, you need to set the tone of treating everyone consistently and fairly. This means that work standards are applied to everyone, including you, and that bullying or discrimination are outlawed in your organization.

Secondly, you need to set the tone for common courtesy. Greeting people when you start work, saying please and thank you are simple behaviours, but they make a significant difference to how people feel about their work.

Thirdly, you need to take account of people's individuality and respect their differences. This means that you set an environment that allows for individual differences, so long as work standards are met. These differences may range from someone who has a desk constantly piled high with papers to someone who follows particular religious practices.

Fourth, you need to show respect for everyone's contribution to the achievement of your goals. The person who keeps the work area clean, or who fits the widget to the machinery, is a vital component of the overall success and needs to be made to feel that their contribution matters.

---

I was asked to investigate the low morale in a particular office environment and to suggest possible solutions. I observed what went on for a few hours and then interviewed the office staff.

The main theme of what they told me was that they felt 'put down' by management. Examples included a lack of please and thank you for the work they did, not being allowed to take their coffee at their desk, being told off for having a five-minute chat, seeing the two 'favourites' being allowed to get away with poor work standards and being told that if they didn't do the extra work demanded of them they were instantly replaceable.

When I suggested to the management that they could begin to resolve the situation by introducing some simple behaviours as work rules, they were astounded. They had taken it for granted that the staff knew they cared really. After all, they had asked me to go in and investigate. None the less, they agreed to try to consciously make these simple, respectful differences, and after some initial suspicion and scepticism, it did change the spirit of the place for the better.

*What is the level of respect in your organization? Take the four aspects of respect and look for evidence that they are being demonstrated in your organization. In particular, notice how your own behaviour fits the definition of respect.*

## recognition

This motivational factor also consists of more than one element. It includes both the rewards for doing something and the everyday behaviours and policies that recognize people's contributions and individuality.

Rewards certainly encompass such things as bonuses or company shares for tasks achieved to standard, but also mean more ordinary things which any manager could instigate. Whether it be going home early or having a company vehicle for the weekend, people appreciate ways of saying thank you for a job well done, for extra effort, or for doing something no one wanted to do. Even a chocolate bar, or a cup of coffee brought to your desk can make a difference, because it is symbolic that your extra contribution has been noticed.

Recognizing people's contributions can be at an organizational level, with awards for service, or for being 'employee of the month', but the everyday level is important. This means simply saying thank you, noticing someone's progress, or as one manager said to me, remembering to make a comment to the person who is never absent. We all respond positively to a 'pat on the back' and just to someone noticing what we are doing, even if it is nothing special.

Organizations can recognize individuality through such policies as parental leave or flexible benefits or career breaks. Again, though, the everyday level of recognition is important. A birthday card, acceptance of a different way of achieving a task, remembering and asking about their weekend away, all these recognize the individual and make people feel important.

Dave was consistently cited to me as an example of a good people manager. When I asked what made him so good, the type of evidence I was given was that he knew everyone by name, he noticed what you did, he always said thank you, and if he thought you looked fraught, he would bring you a cup of tea.

My favourite response was from the associate working on the line, who said that Dave had made him realize that there were only about twenty people in the world who could do what he did, when he thought that his job was boring and ordinary.

*How do you give recognition to your staff? Over a couple of days, notice what you do well, and any areas where you could enhance the recognition you give.*

## responsibility

If people are to be motivated, they need to feel that their potential is being recognized. The first area of responsibility is for their own job. This is the difference between constant supervision and interfering, and telling people what you want as a result and letting them get on with it.

Then there are the extra responsibilities that are over and above their normal job. No one likes having extra jobs dumped on them, yet most people respond to being given extra responsibility – the difference is how and why you ask them to take it on.

If someone is clearly not being stretched or developed in their work, and they show that they would be willing and able to do more, then you need to find more. This can be a particular project, or one of those responsibilities that all businesses have which need ownership, like health and safety, first-aid, arranging regular meetings, etc. It is important to link the responsibility to either an existing strength in the person, or to their development plan.

Pat was administrative assistant to a director. She believed that she had gone as far as she could in her career, although she often said she wished she were more qualified so she could go further. Her boss noticed how his team often consulted her about how to word reports or presentations, and asked her if she would like to be communications officer for the department. She said that she didn't think she was up to it, but would like to have a go. They sorted out between them a development plan, and she started off with great enthusiasm. A year later, her role was seen as vital to the department and her expert advice was being sought by people outside the department as well.

*How do you motivate people by giving them responsibility? Notice to what extent people are able to take responsibility for their own job, and where they have or could have extra responsibilities.*

## recreation

This may seem a strange category to have under motivation. Yet we all know that we learn more and do things with more enthusiasm when there is some fun involved. Recreation really captures the spirit in which work is undertaken – it feels more like recreation than work.

You need to set the tone that allows people to enjoy being at work. It is based on everyday behaviours – that it's OK to have a laugh, to stop and chat for five minutes, to play the fool once in a while. People are pretty good at making life more fun, if they are encouraged to do so, and far from detracting from their performance, it actually lifts their spirits so that they work with more enthusiasm.

By the way, obligatory social activities as a team are not the way you achieve this. They put people under pressure to join in when they may prefer to be with their families, or just have their own personal time. In my experience, social activities outside work tend to happen when people are enjoying being at work. They are a result, not a cause.

We had to do a massive mail-out from the training centre I worked in. It was a boring job, collating thousands of sheets of paper and stuffing them in envelopes. One of my staff suggested that we all did it together at the end of the day. He brought in a cassette player, put on some lively music, and organized us all into an assembly line. It was so much fun that we all agreed to do all our mail-outs that way, and it took no time at all with six pairs of willing hands.

*How do you introduce fun into your workplace? Look at ways people can enjoy being together while still doing their work, and make sure that short chat breaks and laughter are seen as positive contributions to the work effectiveness.*

# recognizing motivational patterns

Once we have set a generally motivational environment, we can begin to fine-tune to cater for individual differences. Each of us tends to have favourite ways of being motivated, that is, our own blueprint for the circumstances that will prompt us into enthusiastic action.

It is important to recognize the differences between us in our motivational patterns, as they can be complete opposites.

For example, some people tend to move away from something they don't like, others move towards something they do like. If you are a 'move towards' person, you are likely to suggest to someone that their life would be better if they learned this new technology. If they are a 'move away from' person, they are likely to merely shrug their shoulders, until you remind them of how irritated and frustrated they get with their present, rather slow and clumsy software.

Shelle Rose Charvet has written an excellent book on motivational patterns, and gives detailed descriptions of the traits and their implications in the workplace. I will list just a few of the more common ones, to give you a flavour:

- *Proactive – reactive.* Proactive people like to make things happen. They like to show their initiative and innovate, and are impatient to get going. Reactive people prefer to wait until they are told to do something. They like to understand fully and analyse before they act, and they are cautious.
- *Internal – external reference.* Internally motivated people act because they think it's the right thing for them to do. They do not really accept others' opinions. Externally motivated people act because others will be impressed or think it's a good thing. They need feedback that tells them they're doing well.

■ *Sameness – difference.* Some people like to know that what they're going to do is like other things they have done. They will holiday in the same place year after year. Others prefer to do something that is different. They will want to holiday in places they have never been to before.

■ *Independent – co-operative.* Some people prefer to work on their own and achieve tasks solo. Others prefer to work in a team, and have people to bounce ideas off.

These pairings are obviously simplistic. They are two ends of a continuum, and we will not always be at one end or the other. None the less, they do provide some useful guidelines to help us to be aware of our own and others' motivational patterns.

> *As you look through this list of patterns, which categories do you think you fall into? And how would you assess your staff's motivational patterns? Notice in particular where yours differ from theirs. These are the areas where you need to offer motivational factors that may not be obvious to you.*

# using what you know about motivation

In order to use this information about motivational factors and patterns, you will need to apply your attention and listening skills to pick up what matters to others. As with influencing, you need to find out about their river (see Chapter 13), so that you can express what you want them to do in their terms.

In particular, you need to identify the benefits to them of doing whatever it is. We are all selfish at heart, and unless we can see a pay-off for getting involved, we tend to stay on the sidelines.

## using the right language

If you want people to be motivated, don't tell them that they 'ought to' do something, or that they 'have to'. Words like these cause an immediate rebellious reaction in most people at an unconscious level.

The words 'ought, should, got to, have to, must' all imply obligation and duty rather than motivation and enthusiasm. They suggest an external pressure or rule to make someone do something, rather than enabling someone to choose to act. Instead try asking, 'Will you . . .?'

# recognizing where they are

It is important to remember that we all vary in our levels of motivation, depending on the circumstances. It is more difficult to be motivated to perform well if you are starving hungry, or if your home life is falling apart.

Maslow called this the hierarchy of needs. Our basic needs have to be satisfied before we can move on to the higher levels:

- *Physical needs:* food, shelter, etc.
- *Safety needs:* protection from physical danger.
- *Social needs:* relating to others well.
- *Esteem:* personal worth and dignity.
- *Self-actualization:* fulfilling own potential; recognized as a good performer.

This applies at a simple everyday level as well. You will have noticed that you don't get the same level of attention or interest in a meeting if it has run over into lunch-time.

# long-term and short-term motivation

These principles apply at both a short-term and long-term level. It is reasonably easy to enable people to be motivated short term to achieve a particular result, but this tends to be linked to crisis management. For example, a drop in sales may require motivational factors to encourage everyone to make more effort and rectify the shortfall.

However, this doesn't produce the ongoing dynamism and enthusiasm that will make the difference to your organization. For this, you need to pay attention to the motivating factors and patterns on an everyday level, maintaining and developing a motivational environment where people will want to come to work on a Monday morning. (This would also mean that there was far less need for crisis management.)

*Assess the motivational environment in your organization. Use the factors and patterns to help you. What is good and needs maintaining? What could be improved and how?*

# conclusion

Motivating others simply means taking account of what will make a difference to them so that they are motivated and enthusiastic about their work. The pay-off is that your workplace becomes more dynamic and you don't have to spend time pushing people to get results. Continuous improvement, quality, innovation and initiative are natural by-products of a motivated workforce. They don't have to be forced.

# supporting **others**

However good the work environment is, and however much we enjoy what we do, we all thrive even more when we receive individual attention from someone.

The one-to-one work you do with your staff will make a significant difference to how they perform. This is recognized to some extent by the fact that what used to be called 'appraisals' is now subsumed under the title of 'performance management'. However, this title does not make clear the fact that your role is to support rather than control.

## what does 'supporting others' mean?

We are going to explore the different types of one-to-one work you can engage in with your staff. These fall into two categories:

- Formal reviews.
- Informal one-to-ones.

We will look at the general principles that apply to both of them, and then at particular aspects of the different categories.

## why work one-to-one with your staff?

Before we look at the principles of one-to-one work, we need to establish the value of engaging with staff in this way.

I have already said that we all thrive when we receive this sort of attention. Nothing pleases people more than feeling that they have been taken notice of as an individual. This can be at the simple level of just remembering and using someone's name. Obviously, though, if they are people you work closely with, they want more than that.

I have stressed throughout the previous chapters on communicating effectively and managing others, the importance of finding out about the other's world. One-to-ones are the obvious place to both elicit the information and demonstrate your awareness. It is easier to pay attention to someone's world when you are dealing with them on their own and it is easier to customize your communication to suit them when you are working with one individual.

People also open out more when they are on their own with you: they don't have to take into account the reactions of others – always assuming that you have a good rapport with them.

---

Jane was a newly appointed manager in an insurance company. I asked her what had prompted her to set up fortnightly one-to-one's with her direct reports – it wasn't normal practice in that company.

She said that they were immensely valuable to her because she rapidly established relationships with her team and discovered what made them tick. On an ongoing basis, they were her major source of information on what could turn into crises and enabled her to forestall those crises. They were also an opportunity to develop and motivate her staff. She saw them as inviolable diary dates.

---

# the principles of one-to-one work

Any one-to-one work needs to be set within the context of some guiding principles:

1. Integrity of purpose and intention.
2. Confidentiality.
3. Clarity of outcomes.
4. Relationship-building.
5. Enhancement of the individual.
6. 'The customer is always right.'

## integrity of purpose and intention

For someone to gain from a one-to-one session, they need to feel that the session is for their benefit and will not be used against them in any way. They get this message from the way in which you approach it.

You need to clarify in your own mind beforehand what your purpose and intention is in holding this session. For example, you could have a general statement such as: 'I want to use this time to build my relationship with x, and to help her to develop her potential in any way I can.'

## confidentiality

Closely linked to the integrity of your purpose is the principle of confidentiality. This has to be strictly adhered to if the person is to trust you with honest opinions and feelings; without that honesty you lose most of the value of one-to-one work.

The only time that you can break confidentiality is with the permission of the person concerned. If it really feels important to you, for the benefit of that person, to share some information with a third party, then you must argue your case with them and gain acceptance.

## clarity of outcomes

Often people are mistrustful of managers who ask for one-to-one sessions. They make assumptions that they are in trouble and going to be told off or worse, or that they are going to be given extra work. This is because, historically, most people have experienced these outcomes as the main reasons for being called out by their manager individually. You need to be clear what you want out of the session, and what you want them to gain from the session, so that you can put their fears to rest at the beginning.

Notice that your outcomes may be linked to a change of behaviour, or an agreement – some form of clear result, or they may be linked to relationship-building or continuing development – longer-term effects.

## relationship-building

All one-to-one sessions should enhance your working relationship with the person concerned in some way. If we get to know others and give them a chance to get to know us, we build a foundation that enables us to work together more effectively. It gives us the 'shorthand' which means that you don't always have to spell everything out, and the trust and rapport that allows you to sometimes just give an instruction and know that it will be OK.

With friends, we know that the times we are alone together provide the cement of the relationship. Similarly, with work colleagues, you can use one-to-one's to produce the cement.

Notice that building a relationship implies more than just you finding out about their world. You also have to let them into your world, so that they understand you better.

## enhancement of the individual

I have already stated that your purpose should be to help the person to develop. Every one-to-one session is an opportunity to help the person to fulfil their potential. Giving positive and constructive feedback (see Chapter 11), encouraging them to resolve their issues and to suggest ways they would like to develop, and just paying them attention and respecting their world, are all behaviours that can occur in any one-to-one session.

This makes the session feel worthwhile for the individual and also means that you have staff who are constantly developing. The indulgence of letting off steam on your part should be saved for one-to-one's with your line managers or chats with your peers – these sessions are primarily for their benefit.

### 'the customer is always right'

This may be a bit of an exaggeration, but it reminds us that the individual needs to be heard, rather than judged, and that any resolution of issues has to be owned by them, not by you.

In therapeutic terms, this is called being client-centred. You are there to help them to define and make their own moves. Your role is as witness, encourager, rather than leader. You may structure the process, but you do not define the answer.

## applying the principles

When you first begin to have one-to-one sessions with your staff, it is vital to both apply and make explicit these principles. They need to know that these sessions are for their benefit, not a means of disciplining and controlling.

After a while, you will build a relationship where they trust that you are applying the principles. The danger at this point is that you become lax. You need to be disciplined in reminding yourself to apply them until they are completely habitual. The difference the sessions make will then become evident.

---

Terry had become convinced of the benefits of one-to-one sessions since their introduction by his line manager. He decided to do the same with his team members.

He couldn't understand why people were finding excuses not to attend, until I asked him how his line manager had introduced the session to him. Then he realized that he needed to make it clear what the purpose and intent of the sessions were, and make explicit the principle involved. After all, he too had been suspicious at first.

---

*How much do you work one-to-one with your direct reports? Identify the formal and informal sessions you have.*

*To what extent do you apply these principles? Can you improve on this? How will you make the change explicit to your staff?*

# formal reviews

In my opinion, there is no question about whether you have formal reviews with your staff. They are a necessary part of supporting and developing your staff, and are also a vital component in maintaining and developing your business.

They may take a variety of forms: appraisal interviews, project reviews, progress reviews, or just regular meetings. They all come under the heading of formal reviews, because they are regular diary dates for a set time period and they have some form of structure to them. (This does not imply that they are conducted in a formal way.)

Their frequency will depend on the context in which you work and your own and your staff's preferences. Certainly a once-yearly appraisal interview is not enough, however well run. I would think that the minimum number would be one every three months.

## structures for formal reviews

It is important to have a structure for these reviews, so that both sides can prepare and make the meeting time valuable. You can have the same basic structure for all of them. It would look something like this:

1. Review of progress since last meeting.
2. Recognition of achievement.
3. Identification and discussion of present issues.
4. Anything else that needs looking at.
5. Next steps.

By giving a structure to the meeting, you ensure that all aspects of a review are covered and make it easy for your staff to know what to expect and to prepare for it. Where it is linked to a performance management or appraisal system, you probably already have a recording format similar to this structure. The difference will be in the time period you are reviewing.

By the way, annual appraisals are much easier if you have also had interim reviews. You will have a record of what this person has achieved throughout the year, as opposed to tending to focus on the last few months.

## review of progress since last meeting

This is the section that ensures that there is some consistency to the reviews. You check that the next steps from last time were useful and that the person did complete them. If not, then it is important to identify the reasons, from his or her point of view, so that you can make any necessary adjustments.

> It was Jim's third review and he still hadn't devised the customer survey questionnaire which was agreed at his first review. His manager had asked him what was stopping him from doing this questionnaire at the last review, and he had said he was unsure about how to word it. She had suggested he bring a draft to her and they talk it through together. This still hadn't happened. 'What's the problem, Jim?' she asked.
>
> He looked very guilty, then blurted out that he never seemed to have any time to do something like this without being interrupted by phone calls, or queries from colleagues. They agreed that he could have a morning at home the next week just to work on this. Jim was relieved that he'd said what the real problem was, and produced an excellent questionnaire.

## recognition of achievement

I believe in listing this separately, as it is easy to pay attention to issues and obstacles and skip past achievement and progress. Yet most of us want to feel that we are making some 'wins', to be motivated to keep progressing. Under this heading, I would look at:

- next steps achieved from the last review;
- other successes which weren't specifically targeted;
- anything the individual is proud of.

Often, there are small things that deserve recognition, but wouldn't necessarily be classed as achievements. For example, the individual may have kept up to date with their filing for three months now and be proud of having made it habitual.

This is an area where your remarks may help to add to the list. People are often reticent about their successes or contributions, but you can add things, like their proactive role in helping the team to come to a decision.

## identification and discussion of present issues

This is the opportunity for the individual to discuss with you the areas of concern and/or interest that are paramount now and in the immediate future.

It may range from 'I'm worried about x' to 'I would really like to be able to y.' You may have some items you wish to add in here, but your primary role is to ensure that the individual airs his or her concerns and desires and to help sort out what he or she can do about them.

It is important that you also ensure that the discussion does not only centre on obstacles and problems, but also looks at possible developments.

### anything else which needs looking at

This opens up the scope of the discussion beyond its primary focus on work. It gives the opportunity for the individual to ask about wider organizational topics, or to discuss and agree holiday plans. He or she can ask you to clarify something that didn't make sense in the last team meeting, or to talk more about the qualification you mentioned a few reviews ago.

Similarly, you might want to give some information about something that will be happening in the organization which he or she might be interested in, or ask how the relationship with a difficult colleague is going.

### next steps

At the end of the session, you need to help set some form of action plan, which will provide the basis for the start of your next one-to-one session.

You need to review all the areas you have discussed during the meeting and help him or her to decide on priorities for the next period of time. The individual needs to clearly own this stage of the process. You can make suggestions, but it is up to him or her to decide.

What you can do is make sure that the next steps are specific and realistic. For example, if someone says, 'I will speak up more in meetings,' you should encourage him or her to specify which meetings and on what sort of topics. You want it to count as a success next time, so you want it to be realistic.

You also need to ensure that there aren't too many items on the list of next steps. It is much better for morale and motivation to under-promise and over-achieve than to set a large number of actions and 'fail' to meet them all.

## the tone of the sessions

I have already made the point that these sessions should be structured, but not formal in the sense of a formal interview. It is up to you to set a comfortable, relaxed tone to the session.

An informal, quiet environment with comfortable seating works best, but even if you cannot arrange this, you can always ensure that it's possible to get a drink of some sort and that there are no interruptions, physically or by phone, to the session.

Above all, it is up to you to make the individual feel that the session is for him or her and that he or she has control. You can use all the skills discussed in Part III on communicating effectively.

_Assess your own one-to-one formal reviews against the description of the process and tone I have described above. Is there any way in which you could improve on them?_

## getting to know the individual

It may look as if this type of session is so structured and performance-related that it will leave no space for finding out more about the individuals. This is not true.

There is the pre-session chat, where you catch up on holidays, family, etc. This is part of the process of setting the tone, where you make it clear that you are interested in the whole person, not just the work persona. If it is a first session, you can ask to be told a bit about his or her life outside work. Then all the discussions and responses given will tell you about the values and concerns of that individual, if you pay full attention.

# informal one-to-ones

These are the unscheduled sessions with individuals. They may be brief conversations in passing, or over coffee, or they may be times when you need to speak about something specific, or someone asks to speak to you.

Once you have established the right tone to formal reviews, you will find that people want to have conversations with you at other times. In the first place, however, you may need to lead this.

## 'it's just a brief conversation'

Even the shortest of conversations has some significance. You can consciously switch on your skills to conduct a formal review, but then be unintentionally dismissive of the same person in the everyday work environment. This will have a negative impact on the good effect of your other work with that person.

A senior manager in an oil company had become aware of the importance of people management and recognized that it would make a significant difference, but he was still driven by office politics. He introduced formal reviews with his team and conducted them very well, but he did not maintain the same attitude outside the review. He would still walk past those people because he saw someone more 'important' to talk to, and if they asked for time with him outside the formal reviews, he was often 'too busy'.

After a couple of months, his team were as sceptical of his commitment to them as they had been before he started the formal reviews. They did not trust him to maintain confidentiality, regarded their reviews as something they had to do and made them as brief as possible.

His conclusion was that they didn't want his attention, so he reverted to his former practice. He was wrong.

*Notice your own informal contact with your team. Do you remember to apply the principles of one-to-one sessions in all your encounters with them?*

## maintaining your space

You may be thinking that your whole day will be taken up with one-to-one sessions if you practice what I'm preaching. I would recommend that you decide on how much time you will spend on one-to-ones, and set that time aside. The equivalent of between one and one and a half days a week would give a yardstick for most situations.

At first, you may need to be more flexible, to clarify for your team that you regard this as important, but once you have established the precedent, your staff will get used to knowing they can book time with you on Thursdays, for example, and will be more disciplined in their demands.

It is important to make one-to-ones enjoyable and useful for you, so that you maintain a positive and constructive attitude towards them.

# conclusion

Your people are your major source of information and your major means of developing your organization. Giving them individual attention enhances both these results, so it has tremendous pay-offs. What's more it is interesting and reminds you of the vital human element in work relationships.

Time spent on one-to-ones, conducted in the right way, is time well spent. It is in these that you will demonstrate many of the attributes of the 21st century manager, and from these sessions your staff will 'pick up' the behaviours that will make a positive difference.

# counselling **and** **coaching**

In the last chapter I talked about using one-to-ones to support your staff. Within the different one-to-ones you have, there are two basic approaches you are likely to use:

- Workplace counselling.
- Coaching.

These two approaches are not mutually exclusive, but they are different. Both are essentially developmental for your staff, even when they start from a place where remedial action is necessary.

---

Sam was not pulling his weight in the office. His manager decided to tackle the issue with him. Sam was very anxious before the meeting and told his friend that he knew he was in for trouble. He knew he was working poorly, but he was bored with the job, yet didn't want to lose it. What else could he do?

His manager used a mixture of counselling and coaching with him in the session, and he came out looking relieved and positive. His friend asked him how the session had gone. 'I realized that I was making the situation worse for myself, and that I could equally well make it better. She agreed with me that the job could be boring, which made me feel better. She encouraged me to look at how I could stretch myself and make the job more interesting. I feel motivated again, and she says that she will help me to keep going.'

His manager had turned the situation around through the approach she used. Sam was ready to develop.

---

# the difference between workplace counselling and coaching

Workplace counselling is a non-directive approach to resolving issues or encouraging development in employees. You allow them to take the lead in identifying the issue, where they want to get to, and how to get there. Your role is to listen, structure their thought process and help them to work it through.

In coaching, you take a more proactive role. You contribute to identifying the issue, where they need to get to, and how to get there. Particularly in this last stage, you will play an active role in helping them to achieve their target. Let's look at these differences.

# workplace counselling

Workplace counselling can best be defined as helping someone to help him- or herself. It is not the same as professional counselling – that requires lengthy training and the development of particular skills. I think of workplace counselling as being like the help you would give to a friend who had an issue to resolve. It is first-line. If someone has an issue they need more help with, then you would refer them on to a professional.

## being a listener

The most important thing you have to offer as a workplace counsellor is your ability to listen without judgement. We have already discussed this when we looked at paying attention. It is those five levels of paying attention that you need to switch on.

By paying attention, you will notice things about what the person is saying which enable you to help them to find a resolution. If you have in mind a simple structure to the process of paying attention, you can help even more.

## the process of workplace counselling

Before you begin workplace counselling, remind yourself of the general principles of one-to-one work. They all apply to this process. You also need to check your own state. Make sure that you are ready to pay attention to someone and are not distracted by other issues.

## starting with a clean slate

We all have a tendency to make assumptions about how people will behave, what their issues are and what the solution would be. In workplace counselling, it is important that you clear out your pre-judgement.

The easiest way to do this is to set a positive intention and general outcome up in your mind. There is then no space for your other thoughts. It might be something like:

> I want to help this person to find a resolution that suits them. I want to support them in their situation, and help them to learn and develop through the process. I want them to feel that they have some actions they can take to make a positive difference to their situation.

In particular, watch out for the danger of wanting to be too helpful. We often hear someone's problem or issue and immediately think of how to solve it. What we forget when we do this is that:

- this might not be the real problem;
- our solution might not be appropriate for their world.

---

I remember a situation when I was working with adolescents. Charlie was a 16-year-old whom we all liked. She lived at home, and was usually quite quiet.

One day she stormed into my office, obviously upset and angry. 'I want someone just to listen to me!' she said. I sat down with her and waited. 'I'm pregnant!' she blurted out. 'And?' I said. 'Oh, thank you,' she said. 'I want to have it, and I need someone to help me sort out how to do that. I've told two other people so far, and they both immediately started sympathizing and suggesting where I could get an abortion. I was getting so mad!'

Charlie's story and reaction are not unusual. We often jump to conclusions, with the best will in the world, and block the person's need to think it through for themselves.

---

*Think back on a few times when you have solved someone's problem for them – we've all done it! Notice how you might have handled it differently if you had just paid attention. Now remember a time when you did just listen and discovered that the problem and solution were different from how you had interpreted them.*

---

## finding out about the issue

You do need to know what they think the issue is. This applies whether they have a problem or whether it is just about developing on from where they already are.

People usually start by giving you some description of the issue. Pay attention and you will notice that certain things are emphasized in their voice or through their body language. Don't make assumptions about their importance at this point. Simply ask useful questions to elicit more information, such as:

- 'What exactly upset you about that?'
- 'How exactly did he respond?'
- 'Can you give me an example of someone saying the wrong thing?'

Notice that these questions ask for more information without implying any judgement. Starting with 'What exactly', 'How exactly', or 'Can you give me an example of . . .' fills out the description without suggesting any view or opinion. On the other hand, 'Why did you do that?' or 'Did you follow that through?' could imply a judgement or opinion on your part.

I find that when I ask for more clarification, the person begins to explore further his or her own reaction and often identifies the issue as being different from the one previously thought.

---

Peter told me that his boss was always picking on him and that he was fed up with being bullied. I asked him to give me an example of when his boss picked on him. He described what sounded like quite a reasonable request to do something, and then added, 'And, as usual, he sounded like my father.' I asked him what exactly that was like, and his voice became quite abrupt and sharp as he said what his boss had said. Then he went quiet for a moment, and said, 'Really, this is about the fact that my boss reminds me of my father, and I tend to react to him as if I were a naughty child who's been found out.'

Dealing with someone who genuinely bullies you is very different from dealing with your own negative reaction to someone, and requires different solutions.

---

## establishing the outcome they want

Once you both are clear about what the real issue is, you can move on to establishing the outcome the person wants. Although in professional counselling a lot of time may be spent on exploring the issue, in workplace counselling I would recommend that you give most attention to establishing the outcome and how to get there. We do not have the luxury of a year or two of weekly sessions with someone, so we want to reach a resolution as quickly as possible.

There are simple questions to ask, to establish the outcomes:

- So how do you want the situation to be?
- How would you like this to turn out?
- Where do you want to get to?
- If you work this out, what will be happening in six months time?

Again, you might want to ask the 'What exactly . . .' and 'How exactly . . .' questions to clarify what is meant. Remember to check out the effect of their outcome on the person concerned and others, so that the former is clear that it is exactly what is wanted.

> Bill said that he wanted to be qualified as a manager. When he thought further about it, he realized that he would prefer to gain his qualification part-time and somewhere near home, so that his pursuit of his career didn't disrupt the family too much.

## how do they get there?

Once you have helped the person to be clear about the outcome that is wanted, you can begin to plan together how to achieve it. Again, your role is to ask useful questions, rather than provide answers. The sort of questions you might ask include:

- What do you need to do to achieve this?
- What would help you to achieve this?
- How could you make this happen?
- What would make it possible for you to achieve this?
- And what else could you do?

I would always want to use the last question, because if people think of one way of achieving something and it doesn't work, they assume that it is not achievable for them. If, on the other hand, they have thought of alternative strategies beforehand, they will try again in a different way.

If someone can't think of anything, I suggest breaking it down into more manageable chunks and going for a smaller target first. A question like

'What would be a step towards this?' is useful for identifying the smaller chunk.

### turning good ideas into action

Once people have thought through their path for resolving their issue, they need to turn it into action. You can ask them 'What will be your first step?' or 'What will you do now?' to get their brains planning to turn their good ideas into action. Check that they come up with something realistic and achievable so that they begin with a success.

At this point you may also like to ask them if there is anything you can do to help them. When it is workplace issues you are dealing with, you can sometimes smooth the way for them or at the least check with them on their progress.

> *Find two situations where you could apply workplace counselling in the next week, and practise paying attention and using the questions. Choose situations where the issues are not too serious. You could even tell the person that you are practising a different approach and you would appreciate their willingness to be part of the experiment.*

## the advantages of workplace counselling

This process enables people to structure their thought processes, so as to resolve their own issues. The answers they come up with are far more likely to be practical and relevant to them, and they feel in control of the situation.

Your role is relatively simple – you pay attention and ask useful questions. Even if you were the one who raised the issue in the first place, this method produces much better results. It also works extremely well as a developmental tool.

Sometimes, though, someone doesn't really know what to do about an issue. This is where coaching may be more useful than counselling.

# coaching

The purpose of coaching is to help someone to learn more easily, so that he or she improves the standard of his or her performance. Although in coaching the same general principles of one-to-one work need to be applied, your role as coach is to play a more active part in identifying outcomes and to help in achieving them. Whether the person has asked for your coaching or you have identified the need to take more of a lead in helping that person to learn, you can still apply the principles in the same way.

## preparing to coach

As with counselling, it is important to set your frame of mind in a non-judgemental and positive way. In a coaching situation, you also need to prepare yourself further. The person concerned is not performing to the required standard in some way. Whether this is skills-based or behaviour-based, the same things apply.

You need to think through how you would like the person to be – the desired outcome of the coaching – and some alternative methods for helping him or her to learn is needed to achieve this.

It is particularly important that you have alternative approaches to learning available to you. Coaching works when the learning approach suits the needs of the individual. This means that you need to be prepared with alternatives, rather than automatically going for your preferred learning style. It would work for you, but not necessarily for someone else.

## different learning styles

There are many useful descriptions of different learning styles, and at a minimum you need to be aware of the following basics:

- *Auditory:* some people like to be told lots about what they need to learn. They like a description of the process, and often appreciate a list of key words or bullet points to remind them. They take information and 'record' it on their internal tape recorder, to play back as they undergo the process.
- *Visual:* some people like to see what needs to be done. They like demonstrations they can observe, or at the least, flow-charts, diagrams or vivid descriptions which they can picture in their imaginations.
- *Kinaesthetic:* some people can only learn if they actually try it out. They need to have a go and ask questions as they go along.

Most of us actually work with a mixture of these, but will have a predominant way which leads us into the learning experience.

So you need to ask yourself how many ways you can find to enable the person's particular learning style. Can you represent the learning in a diagram, through bullet points? Can you give the experience in a safe environment? Notice that good teachers automatically cover all these angles, to cater for differences.

*Think of the last time you coached someone. Did you cater for that person's learning style, or did you just use the method by which you had learned?*

# the first coaching session

In the first coaching session, you need to:

- agree the outcome of the coaching;
- agree the rules of coaching;
- set up the appropriate method of coaching;
- establish a timetable for achievement.

## *agree the outcome of the coaching*

Whether you have decided to coach the person or the person has asked for it, the prompt is likely to have been the identification of some form of under-performance. This means that the problem has been identified, but not how you want things to be.

I have already suggested that in your preparation for coaching you need to think about the outcome you want. Once in the session, you need to make sure that you both have a shared understanding and agreement on what exactly you are aiming to achieve. 'I want you to be better organized' is not good enough. It could mean a tidier desk, the filing done more often, punctuality in attending meetings, etc. Use questions and examples to set a specific outcome, and make sure the person is looking comfortable with it. If doubt or anxiety is showing, then he or she is already working towards failure rather than success. You need to reassure them, or maybe lower the target a little, at least at first.

---

Peter had asked me if I would help him to be more patient with his graduate trainees. He knew that he tended to lose his temper with them and that was not productive. When I checked out with him what outcome he wanted from the coaching, it seemed that it was really about not pre-judging their ideas and suggestions as being impractical. So we agreed that he wanted to listen to their ideas properly and find out exactly what they meant before giving his perspective.

He still looked dubious about it, so I asked him what was bothering him. 'I've got ten graduate trainees, and they are always coming up with bright ideas. This will be a real stretch for me,' he said.

I then suggested that he choose one of them as his 'subject' and concentrate on developing his attention skills with just that one. He immediately looked more comfortable and said he was sure he could do that.

---

## agree the rules of coaching

When you enter into a coaching relationship with someone, you need to make sure that you both see your role in the same way. As well as agreeing the general principles of one-to-one work, you need to agree how you will coach the person.

What does the person need from you as a coach? Does he or she need you to nag, to remind, to encourage, to teach, to review progress? It could be any or all of these, and you need to both understand and be comfortable with the expectations. If you don't want to nag, or teach directly, or whatever, the person needs to know so that there are no false expectations.

Similarly, you need to clarify what is expected of the person being coached. If he or she is expected to practise alone, or read up about the subject, say so beforehand.

## set up the appropriate method of coaching

Once you have agreed your roles in the coaching process, you can sort out the way the learning will be implemented. Here, your preparation of alternative methods will be used. You can offer the person to be coached choices.

The easiest way to establish the best method is to ask for a preference – obvious, but not often done! Questions like 'What would help you to learn from this?' and 'How do you learn things easily?' may elicit the preferred learning style. However, many people don't know what makes it easy for them to learn, so you may need to agree to be experimental with them.

Remember that they also need to feel comfortable with their coach(es) – it may be the right approach with the wrong person.

---

Mike's performance reviews with his staff were in need of improvement. The obvious way to improve was by observing his own manager conduct reviews, since his preference was to see how others did it. This did not seem to be helping. I suggested that he arranged to sit in with three or four different experienced managers. He came back from this saying that he would like to sit in with Jane a few more times, and then have her sit in with him while he did his reviews. He had found himself a coach he was more comfortable with.

---

You may be directly coaching the person, or you may be simply managing the process, making sure that he or she has access to what is needed for learning. Either way, be prepared to offer a mixed package of approaches and to change the package if it isn't working.

## establish a timetable for achievement

In some coaching situations there is no need for a timetable – it happens on the spot. With others, you need to set up a programme:

- When the learning will take place.
- When you will review the learning progress.
- When and how you will check that the learning is achieved.

Even with on-the-spot coaching, I would suggest that you need the last part of the programme at some point, to ensure that the learning has become custom and practice in the workplace and to give the person being coached positive feedback on his or her achievement.

This may sound complex, but it is likely to fit quite simply into the process for formal reviews (see Chapter 15).

## ongoing coaching

Always remember to follow up on coaching, even if it was a one-off situation. People put learning into practice when they have positive feedback that someone is interested in their progress.

They also usually need some reinforcement to turn the newly learned behaviours into habit, and may need some encouragement to overcome initial problems with implementation. Your role as coach is to encourage, support and help them progress with their learning.

## coaching as a process

As a manager, you may not be acting directly as coach to your staff. Every one of you needs to be using the coaching process to help your staff to develop their skills and abilities. Identifying the outcome, the appropriate method of coaching, and maintaining the process are vital skills to develop as part of your portfolio.

*Compare your coaching process with your staff with the one described above. Are there any ways in which you could improve it?*

## conclusion

In the course of your one-to-one work with your staff you are likely to use a mixture of these two approaches to development. Be sure that you distinguish between them, in your own mind and with the person concerned.

The counselling approach, despite its title, is the more empowering form of development. It enables people to have control of their own process for development or resolution of an issue. With coaching, you take a more active role in helping them to develop.

When both these approaches are used well, people become more and more able to use the processes for themselves. You just become the witness or facilitator. You are helping them to develop the skills of how to develop themselves and resolve their own issues by applying these processes consistently – they are learning about learning. As the 21st century manager, you are becoming the resource rather than the director of their development.

# letting **them get on with it**

One of the characteristics of traditional managers is that they are very 'hands-on'. They hold all the strings, manage every project, and control people's activities and behaviour.

---

Jim had just retired after 49 years at work, 27 of them spent in management in a major manufacturing industry. I asked him how it felt to let go of that responsibility. 'It is such a relief to put the burden down,' he said. 'Management is like trying to control an unruly family. You have to watch them all the time, or they don't do the work, or overspend on the budget, or disrupt in other ways. It was easier in the old days, when you had only a small team and one major project to oversee, but in recent times, I had over 40 people and five different projects. It was driving me crazy.'

---

The sheer pressure of an increased workload is forcing managers to rethink their role. It just isn't possible to continue with a hands-on control style with the extra staff and projects managers are now likely to be responsible for, and not everyone can retire!

But there are sounder reasons for changing the style. The description given above by Jim demonstrates the failings of the old style. If you treat your staff like an unruly family, you are likely to have a group of 'rebellious adolescents'. If you want your business to thrive, you need a team of mature adults who will be self-motivated and show initiative and enthusiasm.

All that we have discussed so far is about how to make the changes, in your own attitudes and behaviour and in the way you manage others, that will lead to a different culture in the workplace. The final step in this process is to enable your staff to get on with the job by letting go of the old forms of control.

# making space for people

Most of your employees will have some history of being 'the rebellious adolescent' at work. They will have been managed in a controlling way, pushed rather than influenced, made to conform rather than encouraged to use their individuality. If you were to suddenly let go of the reins, your worst fears of losing control would probably be realized.

The wise manager concentrates on the development of his or her staff, so that they 'grow up' in the workplace and gradually realize that the mature adults they are outside work is also acceptable and indeed welcome within work. Their potential for contributing to the business is enormous, and your job is to gradually make the space for their contribution to expand, rather than overwhelm them by offering all the space at once.

# delegating effectively

The first stage of delegating effectively is to assess what it is appropriate to delegate. This will have factual criteria which relate to whether the person concerned has the required skills and authority to undertake the task or responsibility. On top of that, there are more subjective criteria to consider: is this something you are prepared to let go? And is the person ready to take on this responsibility?

We often ignore the 'emotional' readiness of both sides, yet this is crucial to effective and successful delegation.

---

Tom was aware that it was important to delegate to his team. He knew that Pam was perfectly capable of managing the project on transferring the office technology to a new system, so proposed to her that she take it on. She was delighted to be given a task that would stretch her a bit.

But Tom was very attached to this project – it was his 'baby' – and he kept wanting to know details of what Pam was doing and suggesting what she should do next. Pam felt more like a 'gofer' in the project than its manager, and became very frustrated. After a few weeks of this, she said that she felt that she couldn't do the task and asked Tom to take it back. He was disappointed in her, but glad to have control again.

---

*Have you ever delegated something when you or the other person weren't ready? Notice the effect when this happens.*

# defining results, standards and parameters

When you delegate, you let go of some of your control. If you define the task down to the *n*th degree, this is not delegation, it is giving someone a task – he or she is deputizing for you and doing it in your way. There is no real responsibility being handed over.

However, if you give no definition to the task or responsibility, then you are almost guaranteeing that the person will fail. What he or she needs to know is what results you want, what standards you expect, and what the parameters of the responsibility are.

*Results* are the output from the responsibility, such as monthly reports for the team, or the task completed by the end of the week.

*Standards* are the criteria of successful completion, such as health and safety guidelines complied with, or reports given under all five headings identified. Be careful with standards. We often give too little or too much information in this regard. Too little information is when we take it for granted that someone will realize that the health and safety guidelines need to be complied with, because we check for that automatically. Too much information is when we tell the person how we would do it, and lay down our process or procedure as being the only way to do it.

The *parameters* of the responsibility are essential information to give. If there is a point at which the decision needs to be agreed with you, say so at the beginning. If someone else has a similar responsibility, then make sure that they both know the boundaries. As with standards, you need to check out that the parameters you lay down are genuinely necessary, and are not merely a means of you holding on to control.

*Look at a responsibility you have delegated or are about to delegate. Have you clarified results, standards and parameters in a way that will help the person to achieve the results, without restricting the use of his or her own initiative to get there?*

# monitoring the delegated responsibility

It is important to have some form of follow-up with the person you have delegated to. This is your means of ensuring that he or she is comfortable with the responsibility and of showing continued interest and positive support, without interfering. It makes the difference between delegating and dumping.

You need to approach the monitoring with some sensitivity. You don't want to give the impression of not trusting the person or of trying to take back control. It is worth agreeing, as you delegate, how and when you will review the responsibility, and then apply the principles and process of a review meeting. Sometimes it can be quite informal and quick, other times it will be more structured, depending on the size and complexity of what was delegated.

Monitoring gives the person a chance to air any concerns, clarify any unclear points, and feel recognized for what he or she is doing. It also gives you the opportunity to ensure that the responsibility has been delegated successfully and to rectify any misunderstandings that could limit the achievement for the individual.

*How do you monitor responsibilities you have delegated? Identify one or two and check that you have monitored effectively.*

# the benefits of delegation

Being an effective delegator has great pay-offs for you, your staff and your business. It is a skill well worth developing.

## benefits for you

You have more time and attention to devote to ensuring that the business direction and strategies are appropriate. You can maintain the overview rather than getting caught up in the day-to-day.

You also have more time and attention to give to your people management, supporting and encouraging your staff, so that they want to come to work.

Finally, you have the opportunity to learn by seeing the different ways people tackle their delegated responsibilities. Managers often tell me that they have learned new approaches to old tasks from letting others do them and from seeing them from that fresh perspective.

## benefits for staff

Effective delegation is empowerment in practice. When staff are given responsibility in a clear and defined way, with the intention of enabling them to handle it successfully, they feel valued, recognized and empowered.

It is also a powerful form of staff development, helping them to use and extend their skills and increase their employability. It increases their interest in the job, particularly since most of what you will delegate could be seen as 'management' responsibilities, and are an extension of their job rather than more of the same.

> Mary is part of a project team working on technological developments for the company. She was used to being given a set of tasks to do as part of a project. Her manager had a project to complete for the business that could be done by one person. Instead of telling her what to do, he talked her through the project and asked her if she would like to manage it as well as implement it.
>
> She was over the moon. She scoped the project, budgeted it, set her own time-scale, and produced an excellent result.
>
> When I asked her what difference it made to her, she said, 'I was trusted to manage myself, and proved to myself and to my manager that I deserved that trust. Now I think I could be a project manager on a larger scale.'

## benefits for the organization

Delegation means that more people develop skills that will be of use to the organization, and that different approaches are identified and utilized which can contribute to continuous improvement of the process and products.

There is also a higher motivation level in the company and more commitment from employees to best performance. When people feel they own a process, they tend to give more to it.

## problems with delegation

It is important to recognize that not only do we have to develop our skills in delegating, but we also have to revise our beliefs and attitudes to be able to be effective in this area. There are three areas in particular that we need to look at:

1. What power means.
2. Knowing the 'right' way.
3. Dealing with people's diversity.

# what power means

Traditionally power is equated with control. Empowering others through the delegation of responsibility and decision-making may feel like losing your power and so limit the extent to which you are willing to do it.

You need to consciously redefine your power, to release your grip on the reins of control. As a 21st century manager, your power is based on being the resource that enables things to happen, rather than on being the doer. You are the oil that keeps the machinery working effectively, an invisible yet vital component, because without it everything grinds to a halt.

Two aspects of the shift in working practice make this easier. One is the emphasis on results rather than actions. More and more the question will be 'Did it happen?' rather than 'Have you done it?' Linked to this is the emphasis on teams and co-operative working, rather than individual achievement. By having everyone contribute from their strengths, you achieve the synergy that results in high performance. Your role in this synergy is to continually develop your ability to identify, develop and use the strengths of your team, to act as the catalyst. Achievements are then 'ours' rather than 'mine'.

> Henry, an IT director, described to me the achievements of his team over the 18 months he had been in charge of it. 'I am proud of myself for selecting some very different team members, and for encouraging them to use their different skills. As a result, we are now seen as an effective force in the business. My team members are consulted by business units when they have a problem, and seen as valuable consultants. I am not the expert, but I made it happen and am delighted that we are so highly thought of.'

*Do you talk about what 'we' have achieved, rather than what 'I' have done? Can you be pleased with your invisible power, rather than having to hold on to the reins? Think about ways in which you can reinforce the concept of having an enabling power, rather than a controlling power.*

# knowing the 'right' way

All of us like to be right. We have, over time, developed our own custom and practice and we come to take it for granted that this is the best way to do things. Whether it be how we organize our files or how we manage a project, we establish our own pattern and will justify its use if we are challenged about it. This is why continual improvement is a difficult concept to introduce into organizations. We are not used to challenging our own custom and practice, nor that of the workplace.

As an external consultant, who has not been absorbed into the culture of a particular organization, I often spot practices that seem nonsensical to an objective eye. When I question them, people will either justify them or even agree with me that they are nonsensical, but just say, 'That's the way we do things here.'

To delegate effectively, you have to let go of your script for the way things are done. This can be hard if you are not able to stand back from your ownership and be the learner that we talked about in Part I. Our instinct seems to be to say, 'That's not how you do it!' as soon as we see someone doing something differently from the way we do it, and we rush in to be helpful and correct them.

Yet all great inventions and innovations, all quantum leaps forward, have come from people who didn't accept the taken-for-granted rules of how you do it. One of the great benefits of delegating responsibilities is that it is a good way to find new and more efficient ways of doing things, because someone with a fresh perspective is looking for a way to achieve the desired result.

This doesn't mean that you must never intervene if someone is tackling a responsibility differently from you. Sometimes they *are* going about it the wrong way. But you need to be very careful to ensure that you aren't just imposing your way.

When someone tries a different way, start by being curious rather than judgemental. How are they doing it? What made them decide to try it out this way? How is it working better than your way? How is it not working as well? If you can explore with that person the pros and cons of the two different approaches you may, between you, come up with a third way that is even more effective.

If you are not so busy being 'right', you open up the possibility of learning and development, for you, for the other person, and for the organization.

> An experienced cell manager in a major manufacturing company was asked to find ways to improve the process in his cell. He decided to delegate this to the team leaders. They got together with their teams and talked about what they could try out.
>
> The next day, two of the teams had swapped places on the assembly line. The manager was panicking – this wasn't how they did it! Then he calmed down and decided to see what happened. Within hours, it was evident that the cell was working more effectively. When he asked the team leaders how they came up with the idea, they replied, 'Those of us who have done these jobs have known for ages that this way round would work better, but we weren't allowed to change it.'

*Think of an example where you have to follow custom and practice, yet know that there could be a better way to achieve the same result. How can you influence the custom and practice? Now think of a couple of examples where you impose your 'right' way. Who might have an idea for a better way? Can you delegate to them?*

## dealing with people's diversity

Linked to letting go of the need to be right is the importance of truly accepting people's diversity. Although we may accept intellectually that we are all different and the differences are valuable, it is harder to accept emotionally. We have been brought up with stereotypes and pressure to conform and tend to find it much easier to deal with people who are 'like us'.

There are so many ways in which others may differ from us: gender, race, beliefs, values, background, education, physical and mental ability, state of health, way of thinking, way of behaving, appearance and dress – the list is never ending. Some of these we will find easier to deal with than others, depending on our personal prejudices. The tendency, therefore, will be to delegate to certain people and not to others, not because of their abilities or potential – although we would give that as the reason – but because of our prejudices.

Yet the potential of all our people needs to be realized if we are to have a thriving business. People soon notice when they are being missed out or neglected, and build resentment which can emphasize the very reasons you had for not delegating to them in the first place. It is a vicious circle that you need to break.

First of all, remind yourself of the value of differences. If we all were the same, there would be no learning or development. It is comfortable some of the time to be with 'people like us', but it also becomes boring and routine if we are all predictable.

Secondly, switch on your curiosity rather than your judgement. Find out about this person's world and what matters in it. He or she can give you valuable information that will make it easier for you to work together. You may even find out that you have something in common after all.

Thirdly, identify a strength or potential strength this person has that would contribute positively to the team, and find a way of using that strength.

Fourth, recognize the development for you in finding ways of dealing effectively with someone you find difficult. Experiment with what might work, ask others how they manage such people and treat it as an opportunity to grow in tolerance and understanding.

I have come across many examples of good practice in this area. Here are three of them.

Jackie was the one female team leader in an all-male cell. Her manager and fellow team leaders thought her emotional and 'soft', and tended to be dismissive of her. Another cell manager asked if she could be moved across to his cell. He asked Jackie if she would be the 'guinea-pig' for learning about conducting the new performance review system in the cell. She went to the development workshops, implemented the system with her team, and set the example for the other team leaders with her sympathetic yet firm attitude.

Within Graham's team, there was a well-known troublemaker. He was known as the bullet-maker, because although he was the instigator, he was never seen to 'fire the bullets'. Graham decided that this man could clearly lead and motivate, as he managed to persuade others to do the firing of the bullets for him, so gave him responsibility for the team achieving their financial targets.

Susan was known as the negative one in the team. Whatever anyone came up with, she would always identify reasons why they couldn't do it. She was instrumental in bringing down the morale of the team in a difficult period, and was being ostracized. Her manager asked Susan if she would take a specific role in the team. She asked her to play devil's advocate and then to help identify possible ways around the obstacles she could see. When any idea was to be discussed, she was to contribute in that role. It was agreed with the rest of the team. Susan soon became seen as a valuable contributor to the team as her negativity turned into constructive criticism.

We won't always succeed in turning someone around, but if we delegate effectively according to his or her strengths, then the number of 'difficult' people we have to deal with diminishes dramatically.

*Who do you find difficult to deal with? How could you better use their strengths?*

# conclusion

Delegation is essential if we are to develop a different management style. It requires both a structured process and a shift in our attitude about power and people's ability to contribute to be effective.

With effective delegation we are freed up to concentrate on the areas where we can make the most difference as managers. Without it, our version of 21st century management can only be limited.

# endpiece

## and if it's not working

People management is a complex business – someone described it to me as being like trying to herd cats! There are times when all the good strategies in the world won't work and we need ways of coping with that. I suggest the following:

▨ *Check the person's state*: sometimes they are already in a bad state about something else entirely and no amount of good practice on your part will make the difference. Suggest to them that you both try again at some better time for them.
▨ *Recognize that you may not be the best person to deal with them:* I do believe that we can have personality clashes and there are some people we don't work well with. Is there an alternative?
▨ *Remind yourself of your successes:* it is important not to let one failure throw you off balance – keep it in perspective.
▨ *Ask the person concerned what would work for them:* remember that they probably know better than you what they need to make the situation work more effectively; never be afraid to ask directly.
▨ *Go and do something else:* maybe you are not in the right frame of mind to handle this particular issue. Do something that doesn't involve people for a while and give yourself a break.

# Part V

# The Rest of the Journey

We have looked at the major areas where managers need to develop their abilities and attitudes, if they are to be leaders of successful companies in the 21st century. I made the point in Chapter 8 that it is essential that you become an excellent learner. As such, you will know that even if you can rate yourself highly on all the different areas we have covered, you have still only just begun the journey.

These skills and attributes do not have a boundary on their development – they are not finite learning. We can all become even more skilful in our application of them, and both we and our organizations will benefit from that ongoing development.

In this last section we look at ways you can support yourself and your staff in that development.

# continuing **to develop**

We have already explored some aspects of learning in Chapter 8. However, I would like to go back to this theme because it is central to your development as a 21st century manager. In the 21st century everyone will need to be a continuous learner. We all need to revise our ways of thinking about learning and approaching learning. Our history has linked learning to connotations that are not useful:

1.  Learning requires hard work and hard thinking.
2.  Being a learner is a risky business as we may well fail.
3.  Learning something means adding something new to your repertoire.

If we stop and look at our actual learning through life, we discover that all three are myths.

> 1. Most of our learning has been relatively easy, and much of it has happened without our even realizing it! Most of the difficult parts have been associated with formal teaching situations, which raises questions about whether learning is difficult, or teaching sometimes makes it difficult. As Quentin Crisp once said, 'There can be a wide abyss between teaching and learning.'
>
> 2. Fear of failure may stop us from attempting to learn, but when we review all our learning we discover that we have succeeded more than we have failed. Furthermore, some of the so-called 'failures' have been very useful learning experiences themselves.
>
> 3. Most of our key learning has been developmental rather than new. Although, of course, we do learn new things sometimes – a new skill or tactic – a lot of the time we are building on and adding to or honing what we already know. Wisdom is the accumulation of learning from experience, not a whole repertoire of new skills.

So we need to look at how we can develop ourselves most effectively, using our awareness to consciously use the positives we can associate with learning.

# defining your development

Before deciding what to develop in yourself, you need to decide how you want your development to be. If development *per se* is not appealing to you, emotionally as well as intellectually, it will be one of those good intentions that the path to hell is paved with! It is amazing how often I am told that people don't have time to develop themselves, although they would like to. My belief is that they still attach too many myths to learning. Once development becomes an appealing option, it is also a compelling one and we find ways and means of fitting it in.

Development needs to be challenging and stretching, to take us beyond our routine, yet not so far as to be difficult. In martial arts, they talk about our 'soft limits'. The soft limit is how far you can stretch or bend your body without losing your balance. It is called 'soft' because it is not a fixed limit and you can always extend it by gently pushing the boundaries. I find this a useful metaphor for development. It is a way of extending my soft limits without going too far and losing my balance.

It is also important to remember the implications about learning that come from re-examining the myths. For example, I may decide that I want my development to be relatively easy for me, using my preferred ways of learning. I may want to expand my strengths and interests, rather than concentrate solely on weaknesses, or try and find something new. And I may decide to look for the learning in any 'failures' or 'mistakes' and treat them as part of the development rather than an obstacle.

*What is your definition of your development? Write it out in your own words, saying how you want it to be.*

# different methods of development

There are so many different ways in which we can learn that we can find an appropriate method for anyone's preferred learning style, any subject, and any amount of time or effort we have to give it. I will just run through the main options with you, to remind you of the choices and their benefits.

## traditional training programmes

By 'traditional training programmes' I mean classroom-based programmes with a trainer leading the class. These may be organized within your organization, or externally, with participants from other organizations.

Such programmes are useful to provide a new stimulus or give new information. External programmes keep you in touch with the bigger picture of what is happening in the business world and can, as a by-product, give you useful contacts to enhance your network. Internal programmes can be a useful way to spread a particular working practice or skill throughout the organization. Both give you the chance to share your learning with others in interaction with the rest of the group.

You need to ensure that the programmes are designed and implemented in a way that will give you the results you want. Do you prefer an expert, or an expert facilitator? Do you want to be inspired or instructed? Do you want to explore the practical implications or just learn about the concepts? By checking out that it matches what you want from it, you can ensure that the learning experience is valuable to you.

## technology-based training

This is becoming more and more popular as improved learning packages are being produced specifically for this approach. Its advantages are that you can follow the programme at your own pace and at times to suit you. It is particularly appropriate if you need to improve your information technology skills.

## books, audiotapes and videos

Although sometimes these products are interactive, they are primarily informative. Their advantage is that you can use them at a pace and time to suit you. They are a great way to stretch your ideas and look at things from a different angle.

## coaching

If you want your learning to be personalized and directly relevant to you, then this is a great choice. You may choose a coach who is external to the organization, or someone who can help you to learn in a particular area inside the organization. His or her role is to help you develop in the way you want to develop, and because it's one-to-one it is intensive and can be set up to suit your needs perfectly.

## modelling

This is the best way to learn behaviours and attitudes you admire in others. By observing them, copying them and adapting what you learn to suit you,

you learn quickly and easily. Modelling involves you in finding and observing best practice and is a good way to continually develop your abilities.

## experimentation

Another type of less formal learning is experimentation. Trying out a different behaviour can be fun, and if you allow yourself permission to not necessarily get it right first time, it can be a useful way to learn.

## teaching others

This is a good way to really clarify your own best practice. It helps you to hone your skills because you have to consciously work out the processes or procedures you use to get a good result.

## action learning

This is where you work with a group of peers on enhancing your skills through focusing on a particular work issue. You ask each other questions, bring different perspectives to the issue and develop a synthesis which is better than any of your individual ways of resolving the issue. Learning from and with peers can be a powerful form of cross-fertilization.

## work shadowing

This is literally spending time with someone who is getting on with their job, with opportunities to ask questions to find out more about their reasons for taking certain actions or what led them to a particular decision. It is a valuable way to extend your awareness of others' roles and functions, or how others do a similar job to yours. It is also valuable to the person that you are shadowing, as your questions will make them think about the things they take for granted.

# choosing your development methods

When you come to decide on how you will develop yourself further, you need to look at:

- what you enjoy about learning;
- methods that suit your desired outcomes;
- what will easily fit into your schedule.

## what you enjoy about learning

If your development plan looks like hard work to you, you will find reasons to put off doing it. After all, as a busy manager you can always find other immediate priorities, so make sure that the plan is attractive to you and will motivate you. Ask yourself some of the following questions:

- Do I like learning on my own or do I prefer learning interactively with others?
- Do I like exploring concepts and principles or do I prefer practical learning experiences?
- Do I like a 'teacher' or do I prefer to find out in my own way?
- Do I enjoy reading, or listening, or watching videos?

You may find you like a mixture of methods, in which case you can explore several methods to maintain your interest. It is vital that the learning looks like fun to you, so really consider the options carefully from that point of view.

*When have you really enjoyed learning something? What methods did you use? Ask yourself the questions above, and list all of your preferred methods. Look back at your answers to the similar question in Chapter 8 and build on it.*

## methods that suit your desired outcomes

Once you have identified the ways you like learning, you need to consider what sort of development you want. If you want to understand more about a particular area, that will require different methods to changing your behaviour or developing a particular skill.

> David enjoyed reading and had embarked on a major review of the latest books on management. 'They have made me think', he said, 'and I'm more aware now of what I want to be like, but they didn't tell me how to get there.'
> I suggested that he identify two or three areas in which he now wanted to develop, and then used coaching or workshops to help him to practise the skills.

You also need to consider whether it is important to you to have some form of official qualification or certificate, or if you just want to learn. This depends on your preference – do you want official recognition for your development, or do you want to develop for your own satisfaction? It also depends on whether you enjoy the more academic discipline of a qualification, or whether you prefer to do it in your own way.

## what will easily fit into your schedule

However inspired you are to develop yourself, you need to be realistic about what's possible for you. Your development is not supposed to put extra pressure on you; it is supposed to stretch you and challenge you without being a breaking point. Remember the 'soft limits'. If you design a plan that is achievable and enjoyable, you will find that you automatically begin to extend the soft limits, because learning has become part of your way of life.

Consider how much time you can give to formal learning in a month, and then notice how you can add to your formal learning by consciously practising skills and behaviours, or by reviewing and learning from your experience on a daily or weekly basis. Once we have a learning frame of mind, we can be learners all the time!

*What time can you give to your own development? Consider it carefully, and make it realistic.*

# use of a mentor

Sorting out all these issues concerning development can be complex, particularly if you haven't done it before. It can help considerably to have someone to discuss it with, who will assist in the devising of your plan. Mentors can fulfil this role and more.

## what is a mentor?

A mentor is a guide, who is further along in the journey of development than you and who will support you in your development. Ideally, mentors should be selected by you, because you need to feel comfortable with them and their skills. They may be from within your organization or from outside. They act as a sounding-board for planning your development, offering suggestions from their own experience and helping you to sort out what exactly you want and how best to achieve it.

They also provide you with the ongoing support and encouragement to help you to maintain your implementation of the plan, through regular review sessions.

The mentoring session is a 'safe place' to take your sticking points and issues to: the mentor will help you to find a way through. It is also a place to take your successes and progress, knowing that your mentor will understand and delight in these with you.

*Do you have a mentor? If not, can you identify someone who could fulfil that role for you?*

## other forms of support

If you do not use mentoring to support you in your development, it is worth considering what else you can do to support yourself. Would your line manager provide some support and encouragement? Do you have a colleague who is pursuing a similar line? If so, you could give each other reinforcement and encouragement. Most of us need some form of support to help us keep going when things seem to stagnate and to reinforce our progress with positive feedback.

*How will you ensure that you are supported and encouraged in your development?*

## putting your development plan together

Do write out an outline of your personal development plan, rather than leaving it as vague ideas in your head. This process will help you to focus and clarify and will give you something to monitor yourself against.

Start by identifying which areas you want to develop. Write them down the left-hand side of a page. Then identify suitable methods for this development, on the right-hand side. Where possible, give yourself choices, or a 'combination' package, using several different methods to build on it. Here is an example:

*Development area*
Managing stress better

*Development methods*
Self-help audiotapes
An external seminar
Modelling x who does it well
Practising the techniques I learn

When you have done this, identify how you will gain support for your learning – a mentor, or someone else who will take an interest.

Now look through your list and identify where you want to start. Which seems to you to be the most important, or maybe the easiest to achieve? It doesn't matter how you choose, so long as it is motivating for you.

Finally, check through your list of methods and identify any actions you need to take to make them possible. For example you may need to start now by identifying a seminar or training programme and applying, even if it isn't for another six months.

*You can now make your development plan and start putting it into action.*

Remember that you have already identified how to be in a good learning state in Chapter 8. Use that state to help you to really enjoy and benefit from your development as it progresses.

# developing your staff

All that I have said about developing yourself applies equally to your staff. You can use the same approach with them and may even choose to act as mentor for some of them, where appropriate.

Remember that being a learner is a vital part of 21st century management, and once you are setting the example, you also need to encourage your staff to grow and learn.

# conclusion

Consciously choosing to continually develop your skills is a marvellous way to keep yourself motivated and interested. However well experienced you are in your job, there are always ways you can extend yourself. The added bonus is that you become even more employable and increase your value to your organization, and also your choices about where and in what field you work.

# conclusion

We are working in exciting times. The world is changing rapidly and so is working practice. It was not so long ago that we were right in the middle of the industrial age – for most of us that is part of our personal histories of work.

It is not easy to let go of our history and recognize that we are moving into a new era, and we will all struggle with it at times. This is particularly true during the period of transition, when there is still plenty of evidence that the old practice seems to be accepted and valued.

What I have proposed in this book is that you can develop good practice as a 21st century manager, within the context of the transition. I am not proposing that we all do what Ricardo Semler did and throw out all the rule books. I am suggesting that you work on developing your skills and abilities as people managers, so that as the rules change and as the systems at work adapt to the new requirements, we are ready to take on the new role.

## review of what this means

We have the opportunity to be at the forefront of a radical shift in the way managers lead. I'll summarize briefly.

### awareness of the changing context

We can keep ourselves up to date with the changes occurring and be aware of the bigger picture. It is easy to get caught up in the day-to-day of your own job, but by being aware of the fact that working practice is changing globally, you can deal more effectively with changes that take place and also maintain a longer-term vision of where you and your organization are going. By doing this, you can play an active part in moving towards the outcomes we need for the 21st century. As David Ulrich says, 'Winning will spring from organizational capabilities such as speed, responsiveness, agility, learning capacity and employee competence.' These are the capabilities we have been exploring.

# managing yourself

No one can be effective as a manager of others if they have not learned how to manage themselves effectively. By increasing your self-awareness and exploring the ways in which you can bring out the best in yourself, you enhance the example you set for those who work with you.

Daniel Goleman has written about emotional intelligence as being a prime requirement for success, rather than straight IQ scores. What we have explored is ways of developing your emotional intelligence and using it more effectively at work.

# communicating

We all communicate constantly, both verbally and non-verbally. It is no good being someone who has vision, beliefs and strategies that will help us to move into the new paradigm, if you cannot get your message across effectively.

You also need to be excellent at spotting where other people are at, and working with them to move forward rather than imposing your world view on them and expecting them to come with you. Most people I talk to are beginning to shift their way of thinking about work. They want more quality of life, less pressure, more sense of self-worth. Your job is to harness that and bring benefit to both them and your organization.

# bringing out the best in others

The success of your organization in the 21st century will depend on how your people work. By recognizing what really motivates people to give of their best and by being a powerful resource to help them to develop their skills and abilities, you will make a difference to the success of your organization.

By letting go of the 'control and command' version of management, you will enable others to exploit their potential and realize the true power of being a leader.

# learning, learning, learning

The emphasis throughout this book has been on being a learner. When we are going through a period of transition, those who are at the forefront are those who are using their learning capability.

Both you and your staff will be involved in never-ending change for the rest of your working lives. This gives you the opportunity to continually develop and grow as a person and as a manager.

## what next?

These are exciting times to be living in. As a manager in the 21st century you have the opportunity to make a real difference to the working lives of yourself and all those who work with you. You do not have to wait until someone says that it is time to be the 21st century manager. You can begin to build on your good practice now. All the good practice we have discussed will make a positive difference no matter what stage your organization is at at the moment.

As you worked through this book, I believe that you will have identified lots of ways in which your attitudes and behaviour already match those of the 21st century manager. After all, most of this stuff is just common sense and already proven to work when put into practice. Build on that good practice and use it more and more in your everyday work with others.

There will be some areas where you will have identified ways in which you could improve your practice. Take those which have most appeal for you and do something about them now. Don't put it off until you have time. Make time for small changes now and you will find that you have more time to try other things out.

Also, trust your own intuition. If certain parts of this exploration have jumped off the page at you, then revisit them first – they are obviously the most important for you right now. If some parts have seemed irrelevant to you, don't take my word for it that they are important – follow your own instincts. Being a 21st century manager is being true to the best in yourself, and you can start that immediately, wherever you are on the journey.

The sort of development we have been talking about is not hard work, it is fun. The excellent 21st century manager will look back on the 20th century manager and wonder why he or she put up with so much dissatisfaction and frustration at work, when it was possible to make work enjoyable and challenging.

You have the capabilities. They are inherent in human nature. It's time to get on with changing our working world so that everyone can enjoy their time at work, and free themselves up to have enough energy and time to enjoy the rest of their lives as well.

# recommended
# reading list

## the changing context

All these books give different perspectives on what is likely to happen in business in the near future. Their views differ in some ways, but they all have similar messages.

Bridges, W (1995) *Jobshift*, Nicholas Brealey, London
> A view of the future where no one has traditional jobs.

Hamel, G and Prahalad, C K (1996) *Competing for the Future*, Harvard Business School Press, Boston
> A blueprint for action today to be able to compete in the future.

Handy, C (1990) *The Age of Unreason*, Arrow, London
> A description of a future view of how organizations need to be.

Handy, C (1995) *Beyond Certainty*, Hutchinson, London
> A description of the changing world of organizations.

Handy, C (1997)*The Hungry Spirit*, Hutchinson, London
> His latest book, describing how he feels we need to be in the future.

Naisbitt, J and Aburdene, P (1985) *Re-inventing the Corporation*, Warner Books, New York
> A proposal for how to transform your job and your organization to fit with the information age.

Peters, T (1992) *Liberation Management*, Macmillan, London
> How to deal with what he calls the 'nano-second nineties'.

Peters, T (1994) *The Tom Peters Seminar,* Macmillan, London
> Talks about the changes happening in business and what leaders need to do.

Peters, T (1997) *The Circle of Innovation*, Hodder & Stoughton, London
> His latest book about what's happening in business and how we need to be to deal with it.

Toffler, A (1990) *Powershift*, Bantam, New York
> All of Toffler's books give insights into the shifts happening in society and the need to change.

Wheatley, M (1994) *Leadership and the New Science*, Berrett-Koehler, San Francisco
    Describes the links between developments in science and the way we will need to lead in the 21st century.

# self-management and development

These books offer a variety of approaches to developing yourself, your ways of thinking, and your ways of dealing with others.

Buzan, T (1995) *The Mindmap Book*, BBC, London
    Description of how to use your mind more effectively.
Covey, S (1995) *The Seven Habits of Highly Effective People*, Simon & Schuster, London
    An excellent guide to developing yourself.
De Bono, E (1991) *Handbook for the Positive Revolution*, Viking, London
    Strategies for the 21st century person.
De Bono, E (1996) *Textbook of Wisdom*, Viking, London
    Strategies for developing the way you use your mind.
Dilts, R B, Dilts, R W and Epstein, T (1991) *Tools for Dreamers*, Meta Publications, Cupertino
    Strategies for developing your creativity and innovation.
Dilts, R B and Epstein, T (1995) *Dynamic Learning*, Meta Publications, Capitola
    Strategies for developing your learning skills.
Goleman, D (1996) *Emotional Intelligence*, Bloomsbury, London
    Description of what emotional intelligence is, its value, and how to develop it in yourself and others.
Jeffers, S (1996) *End the Struggle and Dance with Life*, Hodder & Stoughton, London
    Practical guide to keeping yourself in a good state.
Kamp, D (1997) *A Better Guide to Management*, Sound FX Publishing, London
    A set of 12 audiotapes for developing management excellence.
Kanter, R M (1989) *When Giants Learn to Dance*, Routledge, London
    How to be a manager in what she calls the 'post-entrepreneurial society'.
Robbins, A (1988) *Unlimited Power*, Simon & Schuster, London
    A guide to developing your own potential.
Russell, P and Evans, R (1989) *The Creative Manager*, Unwin, London
    A guide to using your mind more effectively.

Senge, P (1990) *The Fifth Discipline*, Doubleday, New York
    Excellent description and practical guidance on developing your skills as a 21st century manager.
Sher, B (1996) *Live the Life You Love*, Hodder & Stoughton, London
    An interesting approach to making your life work for you.

# managing others

Many of the books already listed give guidance on managing others as well as yourself. The ones below are specifically on that subject.

Blanchard, K and Bowles, S (1998) *Gung Ho*, William Morrow, New York
    An excellent description of an approach to turning around the motivation in an organization.
Covey, S (1992) *Principle-centred Leadership*, Simon & Schuster, New York
    A guide to using your values to make a difference.
Heider, J (1989) *The Tao of Leadership*, Wildwood House, Aldershot
    Simple statements based on Taoism which suggest how to lead well.
Kamp, D (1996) *Sharpen Your Team's Skills in People Skills*, McGraw-Hill, Maidenhead
    A manager's guide to improving his or her team's interpersonal skills.
Kamp, D (1998) *Successful Staff Appraisals in a Week*, Hodder & Stoughton, London
    Practical guide to improving your staff review process.

# communication

These books deal specifically with the subject of communication and give practical suggestions on how to improve it.

Charvet, S R (1997) *Words that Change Minds*, Kendall/Hunt, Dubuque, Iowa
    Marvellous guide to how our use of language indicates our motivation, and using that information.
Fisher, R, Ury, W and Patton, B (1991) *Getting to Yes*, Century, London
    Excellent guide to negotiating well.
Laborde, G (1987) *Influencing with Integrity*, Syntony, Palo Alto, CA
    Practical ways of improving your communication with others.
Tannen, D (1992) *That's Not What I Meant*, Virago, London
    Practical guide to improving the way we communicate with others.

## stories that inspire

The books in this list have some common themes that link into the themes of this book. They are lighter reading but will none the less continue your development.

Adams, S (1996) *Dogbert's Management Handbook*, Boxtree, New York
  Any of the books by Adams will remind you why we need to change our style of management.
Bach, R (1973) *Jonathan Livingstone Seagull*, Pan, London
  A fictional story about a seagull who breaks with tradition.
Bach, R (1978) *Illusions*, Mandarin, London
  A fictional story about someone learning to use their full potential.
Brown, M (1989) *Richard Branson*, Michael Joseph Ltd, London
  An authorized biography of Branson.
Chopra, D (1995) *The Way of the Wizard*, Rider, London
  A fictional account of how to develop yourself both emotionally and spiritually.
Harvey-Jones, J (1989) *Making it Happen*, Fontana, London
  His personal reflections on leadership.
Hoff, B (1989) *The Tao of Pooh*, Mandarin, London
  A lovely description of how to be in the world using Pooh stories as illustrations.
Mandela, N (1994) *The Long Road to Freedom*, Little, Brown and Company, London
  His inspiring autobiography.
Redfield, J (1993) *The Celestine Prophecy*, Bantam, New York
  A fictional account of someone discovering how to use their full potential.
Semler, R (1993) *Maverick*, Century, London
  Autobiography of a CEO who took a radical approach to managing his organization.

# VISIT KOGAN PAGE ON-LINE

## http://www.kogan-page.co.uk

For comprehensive information on Kogan Page titles, visit our website.

Features include

- complete catalogue listings, including book reviews and descriptions

- special monthly promotions

- information on NEW titles and BESTSELLING titles

- a secure shopping basket facility for on-line ordering

PLUS everything you need to know about KOGAN PAGE